MW00983722

TO:

_____

FROM:

_____

DATE:

_____

Faith's Checkbook

© 2009 Christian Art Gifts Inc., IL, USA
Christian Art Publishers, RSA

First edition 2009
Second edition 2015
Third edition 2023

Designed by Christian Art Publishers

Images used under license from Shutterstock.com

Scripture quotations are taken from the *Holy Bible*,
New King James Version, copyright © 1979, 1980, 1982
by Thomas Nelson, Inc., Publishers. Used by permission.

Scripture quotations marked KJV are taken from the *Holy Bible*,
King James Version. Copyright © 1962 by The Zondervan
Corporation. Used by permission.

Printed in China

ISBN 978-0-638-00038-2

23 24 25 26 27 28 29 30 31 32 – 10 9 8 7 6 5 4 3 2 1

ONE-MINUTE DEVOTIONS®

Faith's
CHECKBOOK

CHARLES SPURGEON

CHRISTIAN ART
PUBLISHERS

Preface

A promise from God may very instructively be compared to a check payable to order. It is given to the believer with the view of bestowing upon him some good thing. It is not meant that he should read it over comfortably, and then have done with it. No, he is to treat the promise as a reality, as a man treats a check.

He is to take the promise, and endorse it with his own name by personally receiving it as true. He is by faith to accept it as his own. He sets to his seal that God is true and true as to this particular word of promise. He goes further, and believes that he has the blessing in having the sure promise of it, and therefore he puts his name to it to testify to the receipt of the blessing.

This done, he must believingly present the promise to the Lord, as a man presents a check at the counter of the bank. He must plead it by prayer, expecting to have it fulfilled. If he has come to heaven's bank at the right date, he will receive the promised amount at once. If the date should happen to be further on, he must patiently wait till its arrival; but meanwhile he may count the promise as money, for the bank is sure to pay when the due time arrives.

May the Holy Spirit, the Comforter, inspire the people of the Lord with fresh faith! I know that, without His divine power, all that I can say will be of no avail; but, under His quickening influence, even the humblest testimony will confirm feeble knees, and strengthen weak hands. God is glorified when His servants trust Him implicitly. We cannot be too much like children with our heavenly Father. Our young ones ask no question about our will or our power, but having once received a promise from Father, they rejoice in the prospect of its fulfillment, never doubting that it is sure as the sun. May many readers, whom I may never see, discover the duty and delight of such child-like trust in God while they are reading the little bit which I have prepared for each day in the year.

May our Lord Jesus accept my service for His sheep and lambs.

His unworthy servant,
C. H. Spurgeon

January

THE BIBLE'S FIRST PROMISE

"I will put enmity between you and the woman,
and between your seed and her seed;
he shall bruise your head,
and you shall bruise his heel."

~ *Genesis 3:15*

This is the first promise to fallen man. It has been in great measure fulfilled. The seed of the woman was bruised; yet how terrible will be the final bruising of the serpent's head! This was virtually done when Jesus took away sin and vanquished death; but it awaits a still fuller accomplishment at our Lord's Second Advent.

This promise stands as a prophecy that we shall be afflicted by the powers of evil, and thus bruised in our heel: but we shall triumph in Christ, who sets His foot on the serpent's head. This year we may have to learn the first part of this promise through experience, the temptations of the devil, and the unkindness of the ungodly.

They may so bruise us that we may limp; but let us grasp the second part of the text. By faith let us rejoice that we shall still reign in Christ Jesus.

CONQUEST TO VICTORY

*And the God of peace will bruise
Satan under your feet shortly.*

~ Romans 16:20

This promise follows that of yesterday's. We are to be conformed to our covenant Head not only in His being bruised in His heel, but in His conquest of the Evil One.

The archenemy tripped up the feet of the unwary and deceived the hearts of the simple; but he was to get the worst of it and to be trodden down by those whom he had troubled. This victory would not come to the people of God through their own skill or power; but God Himself would bruise Satan. Though it would be under their feet, the bruising would be of the Lord alone.

Let us bravely tread upon inferior spirits and even the Prince of Darkness himself. In unquestioning confidence in God, let us look for speedy victory. "Shortly!" we shall set our foot on the serpent! What a joy to crush evil! By faith in Jesus tread the tempter down.

REST ON A PROMISE

"The land on which you lie
I will give to you and your descendants."

~ Genesis 28:13

No promise is of private interpretation: it belongs to all believers. If you can in faith lie down upon a promise, and take your rest on it, it is yours.

Where Jacob rested, there he took possession. Stretching upon the ground, he little fancied that he was entering into ownership of the land; yet so it was. He saw in his dream that wondrous ladder that unites earth and heaven; and surely where the foot of the ladder stood he must have a right to the soil, for otherwise he could not reach the divine stairway. Every promise is ours if we will but lie down upon it in restful faith.

Use the Lord's words as your pillows. Lie down and dream only of Him. See the angels coming and going upon Him between your soul and God's; and be sure that the promise is your own God-given portion, as spoken especially to you.

IN CALM REPOSE

"I will make them to lie down safely."

~ *Hosea 2:18* KJV

Saints are to have peace. The passage from which this gracious word is taken speaks of peace "with the beasts of the field, with the birds of the air, and with the creeping things of the ground." This is peace with earthly enemies, mysterious evils, and little annoyances! Any of these might keep us from lying down, but none of them shall do so. The Lord will destroy those things that threaten His people.

With this peace will come rest. "He gives His beloved sleep" (Ps. 127:2).

This rest will be a safe one. It is one thing to lie down, but quite another "to lie down safely." It is safer for a believer to lie down in peace than to sit up and worry.

"He makes me to lie down in green pastures" (Ps. 23:2). We never rest till the Comforter makes us lie down.

A WONDERFUL GUARANTEE

"I will strengthen you."

~ Isaiah 41:10

When called to serve or to suffer, we take stock of our strength, and find it to be less than we thought, and less than we need. But let not our heart sink while we have such a word as this to fall back upon.

God has strength omnipotent, and His promise is that He will give it to us. There is no telling how much power God can put into a man. When divine strength comes, human weakness is no more a hindrance.

Do we not remember seasons of labor and trial where we received such special strength that we wondered at ourselves? In the midst of danger, we were calm; in slander, we were self-contained; and in sickness, we were patient.

The fact is that God gives unexpected strength when unusual trials come upon us. My own weakness makes me shrink, but God's promise makes me brave.

HELP FROM WITHOUT

"Yes, I will help you."

~ *Isaiah 41:10*

Yesterday's promise secured us strength for what we have to do, but this guarantees us aid in cases where we cannot act alone. The Lord says, "I will help you." God can raise us up allies in our warfare, but even if He does not send us human assistance, He Himself will be at our side, and this is better still.

His help is timely, His help is very wise, His help is effectual, His help is more than help, for He bears all the burden and supplies in all the need.

Because He has already been our help, we feel confidence in Him for the present and the future. Our prayer is, "Lord, be my helper;" our experience is, "The Spirit helps in our weaknesses;" our expectation is, "I will lift up my eyes to the hills – from where my help comes;" and our song soon will be, "You, Lord, have helped me."

ALWAYS GROWING

"You will see greater things than these."

~ *John 1:50*

This was spoken to a childlike believer who was ready to accept Jesus as the Son of God upon one convincing piece of argument. Those who are willing to see shall see: it is because we shut our eyes that we become blind.

We have seen much already. Great and unsearchable things has the Lord showed unto us, but there are greater truths in His Word, greater depths of experience, greater heights of fellowship, greater discoveries of power, and love, and wisdom. These we are yet to see if we are willing to believe our Lord. Power to see the truth is a blessing. Heaven shall be opened to us.

Let us keep our eyes open toward spiritual objects, and expect to see more and more, seeing greater and still greater things, till we behold the Great God Himself and never again lose sight of Him.

PURITY OF HEART AND LIFE

"Blessed are the pure in heart,
for they shall see God."

~ *Matthew 5:8*

Purity is the main thing to aim at. We need to be made clean within through the Spirit and the Word. There is a close connection between the affections and the understanding: if we love evil, we cannot understand that which is good. If the heart is foul, the eye will be dim. How can those men who love unholy things see a holy God?

What a privilege it is to see God here! A glimpse of Him is heaven below! In Christ Jesus, the pure in heart behold the Father. We see Him; His truth, His love, His purpose, His sovereignty, and His covenant character. But this is only if sin is kept out of the heart. The desire of Moses, "Please, show me Your glory," can only be fulfilled in us as we purify ourselves from all iniquity. Lord, make us pure in heart, that we may see You!

GAINING BY GIVING

"The liberal soul shall be made fat."

~ *Proverbs 11:25 KJV*

If I desire to flourish in soul, I must not hoard up my stores but must distribute to the poor. Faith's way of prosperity is gaining by giving. I must try this again and again; and I may expect that as much of prosperity as will be good for me will come to me as a gracious reward for a liberal course of action.

Of course, I may not be sure of growing rich. I shall be fat, but not too fat. Too great riches might cause me the dyspepsia of worldliness, and perhaps bring on a fatty degeneration of the heart. No, I may well be satisfied and thoroughly content.

But there is a mental and spiritual fatness which I would greatly covet, and these come as the result of generous thoughts toward my God, His church, and my fellow men. Let me not stint, lest I starve my heart. Let me be bountiful and liberal, for *so* shall I be like my Lord. He gave himself for me: shall I grudge Him anything?

DIVINE REWARD

*"He who waters will also
be watered himself."*

~ *Proverbs 11:25*

If I carefully consider others, God will consider me and will reward me. This is the Lord's own promise; be it mine to fulfill the condition, and then to expect its fulfillment.

I may care about myself; I may watch over my own feelings; and I may lament my own weakness, but it will be far more profitable for me to become unselfish and begin to care for the souls of those around me. My tank is getting very low; no fresh rain comes to fill it; what shall I do?

I will pull up the plug, and let its contents run out to water the withering plants around me. What do I see? My cistern seems to fill as it flows. A secret spring is at work. While all was stagnant, the fresh spring was sealed; but as my stock flows out to water others, the Lord thinks about me. Hallelujah!

FAITH SEES THE RAINBOW

*"It shall be, when I bring a cloud over the earth,
that the rainbow shall be seen in the cloud."*

~ Genesis 9:14

Just now clouds are plentiful enough, but we are not afraid that the world will be destroyed by a flood. We see the rainbow often enough to prevent our having any such fears. The covenant that the Lord made with Noah stands fast, and we have no doubts about it. Why, then, should we think that the clouds of trouble, which now darken our sky, will end in our destruction? Dismiss such groundless and dishonoring fears!

Faith always sees the rainbow of covenant promise whenever sense sees the cloud of affliction. Let us be of good courage. Never does God so darken our sky as to leave His covenant without a witness; and even if He did, we would trust Him still, since He cannot lie or in any other way fail to keep His covenant of peace. Until the waters go over the earth again, we have no reason for doubting God.

LOVED UNTO THE END

For the Lord will not cast off forever.

~ *Lamentations 3:31*

He may cast away for a season, but not forever. It is not like the Lord to cast off those whom He loves: for "having loved His own who were in the world, He loved them to the end."

He chose us from eternity, and He will love us throughout eternity. He loved us so as to die for us, and we may therefore be sure that His love will never die. His honor is so wrapped up in the salvation of the believer that He can no more cast him off than He can cast off His own robes as King of glory.

Did you think you were cast off? Why did you think so evil of the Lord who has betrothed you to Himself? Cast off such thoughts, and never let them lodge in your soul again. "God has not cast away His people whom He foreknew" (Rom. 11:2).

NEVER CAST OUT

*"The one who comes to Me
I will by no means cast out."*

~ *John 6:37*

Is there any instance of our Lord's casting out a coming one? There has been none, and there never will be. Among the lost souls in hell, there is not one that can say, "I went to Jesus and He refused me."

Suppose we go to Jesus now about the evils of today. Of this we may be sure – He will not refuse us audience; He will not shut the door of His grace in the face of any one of us.

He receives sinners, He turns away none. We come to Him in weakness and sin, with trembling faith, small knowledge, and slender hope; but He does not cast us out. We come by prayer, and that prayer broken; with confession, and that confession faulty; with praise, and that praise far short of His merits; but yet He receives us. Let us come again today to Him who never casts us out.

REST IS A GIFT

*"Come to Me, all you who labor and
are heavy laden, and I will give you rest."*

~ *Matthew 11:28*

We who are saved find rest in Jesus. Those who are not saved will receive rest if they come to Him, for here He promises to *give* it. Let us gladly accept what He gladly gives; receive it as a gift.

You are heavy laden with sin, fear, care, remorse, fear of death; but if you come to Him, He will unload you. He carried the crushing mass of our sin that we might no longer carry it.

He made Himself the great Burden-bearer, that every heavy-laden one might cease from bowing down under the enormous pressure.

Jesus gives rest. It is so. Will you believe it? Will you put it to the test? If you come to Him, the rest that He will give you will be deep, safe, holy, and everlasting. He gives a rest that develops into heaven, and He gives it this day to all who come to Him.

MADE RICH BY FAITH

For the needy shall not always be forgotten;
the expectation of the poor shall not perish forever.

~ *Psalm 9:18*

Poverty is a hard heritage, but those who trust in the Lord are made rich by faith. They know that they are not forgotten by God; and though it may seem that they are overlooked in His providential distribution of good things, they look for a time when all this shall be righted.

Even now the Lord remembers His poor but precious sons. So the godly poor have great expectations. They expect the Lord to provide them all things necessary; they expect to see all things working for their good; they expect to have closer fellowship with their Lord; they expect His Second Advent and to share its glory.

This expectation cannot perish, for it is laid up in Christ Jesus, who lives forever; and because He lives, it shall live also.

Therefore, let us, when we have short commons below, think of the royal table above.

EVEN THE FAINTEST CALL

*It shall come to pass that whoever calls
on the name of the LORD shall be saved.*

~ Joel 2:32

Why do I not call on His name? Why do I run to others when God is so near? Why do I devise schemes and plans? Why not at once put my burden upon the Lord? In vain shall I look for deliverance elsewhere; but with God I shall find it.

I need not ask whether I may call on Him or not, for "whoever" is a very wide and comprehensive one. Whoever means me, for it means everybody who calls upon God. Therefore at once call upon the glorious Lord who has made so large a promise.

My case is urgent, and I do not see how I am to be delivered; but this is no business of mine. He who makes the promise will find out ways of keeping it. It is mine to obey His commands; it is not mine to direct His counsel. I call upon Him, and He will deliver me.

A MAN WITHOUT FEAR

He said, "I will certainly be with you."

~Exodus 3:12

Of course, if the Lord sent Moses on an errand, He would not let him go alone. It could not be imagined that a wise God would match poor Moses with Pharaoh, the mightiest king in the world, and the enormous forces of Egypt. Hence He says, "I will certainly be with you," as if it were out of the question that He would send him alone.

In my case, also, the same rule will hold good. If I go upon the Lord's errand, with a simple reliance upon His power and a single eye to His glory, it is certain that He will be with me. His sending me binds Him to back me up. What more can I want? If He is with me, I must succeed.

Let me not go timidly, halfheartedly, carelessly, presumptuously. In such company as God I must, like Moses, go in unto Pharaoh without fear.

CHRIST AND HIS CHILDREN

When You make His soul an offering
for sin, He shall see His seed.

~ Isaiah 53:10

Our Lord Jesus has not died in vain. He died as our substitute because death was the penalty of our sins. By death, He became like the corn of wheat that brings forth much fruit. There must be a succession of children unto Jesus; He is "the Father of the everlasting age."

A man is honored in his sons, and Jesus has His quiver full of these arrows of the mighty. A man is represented in his children, and so is the Christ in Christians.

Jesus lives, for He sees His seed. He fixes His eye on us; He delights in us; He recognizes us as the fruit of His soul's work. Let us be glad that our Lord does not fail to enjoy the result of His sacrifice. Those eyes which once wept for us are now viewing us with pleasure. He looks upon those who are looking unto Him. What a joy is this!

MOUTH CONFESSION, HEART BELIEF

*If you confess with your mouth the Lord Jesus
and believe in your heart that God has raised
Him from the dead, you will be saved.*

~ *Romans 10:9*

Have I openly confessed my faith in Jesus as the Savior whom God raised from the dead, and have I done it in God's way? Let me honestly answer this question.

There must also be belief with the heart. Do I sincerely believe in the risen Lord Jesus? Do I trust in Him as my sole hope of salvation? Is this trust from my heart? Let me answer as before God.

If I can truly claim that I have both confessed Christ and believed in Him, then I am saved. The text does not say it may be so, but it is clear as the sun in the heavens: "You will be saved."

I must be saved from the guilt and power of sin. God has said it, "You will be saved." I believe it. I shall be saved. I am saved. Glory be to God forever and ever!

THE OVERCOMER

*"To him who overcomes I will give
to eat from the tree of life,
which is in the midst of the Paradise of God."*

~ *Revelation 2:7*

No man may turn his back in the day of battle. We must fight if we would reign, and we must carry on the warfare till we overcome every enemy. We are to overcome the false prophets who have come into the world and the evils that accompany their teaching. We are to overcome our own faintness of heart and tendency to decline from our first love.

If by grace we win the day, as we shall if we follow our conquering Leader, then we shall be admitted to the very center of the paradise of God, and shall be permitted to pass by the cherub and his flaming sword, and come to that guarded tree, whereof if a man eat, he shall live forever.

Pluck up courage! To flee the conflict will be to lose the joys of the new, better Eden; to fight unto victory is to walk with God in paradise.

GOD'S ENEMIES SHALL BOW

*"The Egyptians shall know
that I am the LORD."*

~ Exodus 7:5

Egypt dared to set up its idols, and ask, "Who is the Lord?" When His judgments thundered over their heads, destroyed their harvests, and killed their sons, they began to discern Jehovah's power.

There will yet be such things done in the earth as shall bring skeptics to their knees. Let us not be dismayed because of their blasphemies for the Lord can take care of His own name, and He will do so.

The salvation of His own people was another means of making Egypt know that the God of Israel was Jehovah, the living and true God. No Israelite died by any one of the ten plagues. None of the chosen seed were drowned in the Red Sea.

Oh, that His convincing power would go forth by His Holy Spirit in the preaching of the gospel till all nations shall bow at the name of Jesus and call Him Lord!

CHRISTIAN LIBERALITY

Blessed is he who considers the poor;
the LORD will deliver him in time of trouble.

~ *Psalm 41:1*

To think about the poor and let them lie on our hearts is a Christian's duty; for Jesus said, "The poor will always be with you."

Many give their money to the poor in a hurry, without thought; and many more give nothing at all. This precious promise belongs to those who "consider" the poor, devise plans for their benefit, and considerately carry them out. We can do more by care than by cash and most with the two together. To those who consider the poor, the Lord promises His own consideration in times of distress.

We shall have a time of trouble, however generous we may be: but if we are charitable, we may put in a claim for peculiar deliverance, and the Lord will not deny His own word and bond. As you have done unto others, so will the Lord do unto you. Empty your pockets.

A COMPLETED SACRIFICE

*He shall put his hand on the head of the burnt offering,
and it will be accepted on his behalf
to make atonement for him.*

~ *Leviticus 1:4*

If by that laying on of his hand, the bullock became the offerer's sacrifice, how much more shall Jesus become ours by the laying on of the hand of faith?

> My faith doth lay her hand
> On that dear head of Thine,
> While like a penitent I stand,
> And there confess my sin.

If a bullock could be accepted to make atonement, how much more shall the Lord Jesus be our full and all-sufficient propitiation? Jesus is accepted for us to make atonement for us, and we are "accepted in the Beloved."

Let the reader lay his hand at once on the Lord's completed sacrifice, that by accepting it he may obtain the benefit of it. Jesus is yours now if you will have Him. Lean on Him.

CARE OF OUR FEET

He will guard the feet of His saints.

~ 1 Samuel 2:9

The way is slippery, and our feet are feeble, but the Lord will Himself be our guardian.

He will keep our feet from falling so that we do not defile our garments or wound our souls.

He will keep our feet from wandering so that we do not go into paths of error or ways of folly.

He will keep our feet from swelling and blistering because of the roughness and length of the way.

He will keep our feet from wounds: our shoes shall be iron and brass, so that even if we tread on the edge of the sword or on deadly serpents, we shall be safe.

He will also pluck our feet out of the net. We shall not be entangled by the deceit of crafty foes.

With such a promise as this, let us run without weariness, and walk without fear. He who keeps our feet will do it effectually.

HE ACTS ON HONEST CONFESSION

*He looks at men and says, "I have sinned,
and perverted what was right, and it did not
profit me. He will redeem his soul from going
down to the pit, and his life shall see the light."*

~ Job 33:27-28

This is a word of truth and it is tantamount to a promise. What the Lord has done, and is doing, He will continue to do while the world stands. The Lord will receive all who come to Him with a sincere confession of their sin.

Can we not endorse the language here used? Have we not sinned, sinned personally so as to say, "I have sinned"? Sinned willfully, having perverted what is right? Sinned so as to discover that there is no profit in it, but an eternal loss? Let us then go to God with this honest acknowledgment.

Let us plead His promise in the name of Jesus. He will deliver us from the pit of hell; He will grant us life and light. Why should we despair? Why should we doubt? The Lord means what He says. Lord, we confess, and we pray You to forgive!

GOD ROUTS FEAR

There is no sorcery against Jacob,
nor any divination against Israel.

~ Numbers 23:23

How this should destroy all silly, superstitious fears! Even if there were any truth in witchcraft and omens, they could not affect the people of the Lord. Those whom God blesses, devils cannot curse.

Ungodly men may cunningly plot the overthrow of the Lord's people; but with all their secrecy and policy they are doomed to fail. They gather together; but as the Lord is not with them, they gather together in vain.

We may sit still, and let them weave their nets, for we shall not be taken in them. Though they call in the aid of Beelzebub, it will avail them nothing. What a blessing this is! How it quiets the heart!

We need not fear the fiend himself, nor any secret enemies whose words are full of deceit and whose plans are for evil. They cannot hurt those who trust in God. We defy the devil and all his legions.

PRECIOUS REPENTANCE

*"There you shall remember your ways and all your
doings with which you were defiled; and you shall
loathe yourselves in your own sight because
of all the evils that you have committed."*

~ *Ezekiel 20:43*

When we are accepted of the Lord and are standing in the place of favor, peace, and safety, then we are led to repent of all our failures. So precious is repentance that we may call it a diamond of the first water, and this is sweetly promised to the people of God as one most sanctifying result of salvation.

A sense of blood-bought pardon and undeserved mercy is the best means of dissolving a heart of stone. Are we feeling hard? Think of covenant love, and then we shall leave sin, lament sin, and loathe sin – we shall loathe ourselves for sinning against such infinite love.

Let us come to God with this promise of penitence, and ask Him to help us to remember, and repent, and regret and return. Oh, that we could enjoy the melting of holy sorrow! Lord, speak to the rock, and cause the waters to flow!

TEARS SHALL CEASE

*God will wipe away
every tear from their eyes.*

~ *Revelation 21:4*

For believers sorrow shall cease and tears shall be wiped away. Now is the world of weeping, but there shall be a new heaven and a new earth (Rev. 21:1) and therefore there will be nothing to weep over.

Read the second verse, and note how it speaks of the bride and her marriage. The Lamb's wedding is a time for boundless pleasure, and tears would be out of place.

The third verse says that God Himself will dwell among men; and surely at His right hand there are pleasures forevermore, and tears can no longer flow. Oh eyes that are red with weeping cease your flow, for in a little while you shall know no more tears!

None can wipe tears away like the God of love, but He is coming to do it. "Weeping may endure for a night, but joy comes in the morning" (Ps. 30:5).

OBEDIENCE BRINGS BLESSING

*"Observe and obey all these words which I command you,
that it may go well with you and your children
after you forever, when you do what is good and
right in the sight of the LORD your God."*

~ *Deuteronomy 12:28*

Though salvation is not by the works of the law, yet the blessings that are promised to obedience are not denied to the faithful servants of God.

We are to note and listen to the revealed will of the Lord, giving our attention not to portions of it, but to "all these words". There must be no picking and choosing, but a respect to all that God has commanded. This is the road of blessedness. The Lord's blessing is upon His chosen to the third and fourth generation. If they walk uprightly before Him, He will make all men know that they are a seed that the Lord has blessed.

No blessing can come to us through dishonesty or double-dealing. The ways of worldly conformity and unholiness cannot bring good. It will go well with us when we go well before God. That which gives pleasure to God will bring pleasure to us.

A HEAVENLY ESCORT

*"Behold, I am with you and will
keep you wherever you go."*

~ *Genesis 28:15*

Do we need journeying mercies? If we go at the call of duty we shall have God's presence and preservation. Why should we look upon removal to another country as a sorrowful necessity when it is laid upon us by the divine will?

In any region the Lord is the believer's dwelling place. When God says, "I will keep you," we are in no real danger. This is a blessed passport and a heavenly escort for a traveler.

Jacob had never left his father's room before: he had been a mother's boy, and not an adventurer like his brother. Yet he went abroad, and God went with him. He had little luggage and no attendants; yet no prince ever journeyed with a nobler bodyguard. Even while he slept in the open field, angels watched over him. If the Lord bids us go, let us say with our Lord Jesus, "Arise, let us go hence."

GOD ALWAYS HEARS

My God will hear me.

~ Micah 7:7

Friends may be unfaithful but the Lord will not turn away from the gracious soul; on the contrary, He will hear all its desires. Even in wretched situations our Best Friend remains true, and we may tell Him all our grief.

Look unto the Lord, and do not quarrel with men or women. If our loving appeals are disregarded, let us wait upon the God of our salvation, for He will hear us.

Because God is the living God, He can hear; because He is a loving God, He will hear; because He is our covenant God, He has bound Himself to hear us. If we can each one speak of Him as "My God", we may with absolute certainty say, "My God will hear me."

Come, then, and let your sorrows tell themselves out to the Lord! I will bow the knee in secret and inwardly whisper, "My God will hear me."

February

NEVER DESPAIR

"To you who fear My name the Sun of Righteousness shall arise with healing in His wings."

~ *Malachi 4:2*

Is it dark with you? Does the night deepen into a denser blackness? Do not despair: the sun will rise. When the night is darkest, dawn is nearest.

The sun that will arise is of no common sort. It is the Sun of Righteousness, whose every ray is holiness. Jesus as much displays the holiness of God as His love. Our deliverance, when it comes, will be safe because of His righteousness.

Do we reverence the living God, and walk in His ways? Then for us the night must be short, and when the morning comes, all the sickness and sorrow of our soul will be over forever.

Has Jesus risen upon us? Let us sit in the sun. Has He hidden His face? Let us wait for His rising. He will shine forth as surely as the sun.

GROW UP

*"You shall go out and grow fat
like stall-fed calves."*

~ Malachi 4:2

When the sun shines, the sick quit their chambers, and walk abroad to breathe the fresh air. When the sun brings spring, the cattle quit their stalls and seek pasture on the higher grounds. When we have conscious fellowship with our Lord, we leave the stall of despondency and walk in the fields of holy confidence, feeding on the sweet pasturage that grows nearer heaven.

To "go forth" and to "grow up" is a double promise. Enjoy both blessings! Why be a prisoner? Arise, and walk at liberty.

Why remain a babe in grace? Grow up. Young calves grow fast, especially if they are stall-fed; and you have the choice care of your Redeemer. Grow, then, in grace and in knowledge of your Lord and Savior. The Sun of Righteousness has risen upon you. Open your heart, as buds to the sun, expand and grow up into Him in all things.

HE FREELY GIVES

He who did not spare His own Son,
but delivered Him up for us all, how shall He
not with Him also freely give us all things?

~ Romans 8:32

This is a conglomerate of promises, a mass of rubies and emeralds and diamonds, with a nugget of gold. It is a question that can never be answered so as to cause us any anxiety.

What can the Lord deny us after giving us Jesus? If we need all things in heaven and earth, He will grant them to us: for if there had been a limit anywhere, He would have kept back His own Son.

What you ask for, He will *give freely*. Of His own will, He gave us His own Son. And because He freely gave His Only Begotten, you can trust your heavenly Father to give you anything, to give you everything. Your poor prayer would have no force with Omnipotence if force were needed; but His love, like a spring, rises of itself and overflows for the supply of all your needs.

HE WILL RETURN

"I will not leave you orphans;
I will come to you."

~ *John 14:18*

Jesus Christ left us, and yet we are not left orphans. Our comfort is that He will come to us, and this is consolation enough to sustain us through His prolonged absence. Jesus is already on His way and none can prevent His coming or put it back for a quarter of an hour. He specially says, "I will come to you," and so He will. His coming is especially to and for His own people.

When we lose the joyful sense of His presence, we mourn; but we may not sorrow as if there were no hope. Our Lord in a little wrath has hid Himself from us for a moment; but He will return in full favor. He leaves us in a sense, but only in a sense.

When He withdraws, He leaves a pledge behind that He will return. O Lord, come quickly!

JUSTICE SATISFIED

*"When I see the blood,
I will pass over you."*

~ *Exodus 12:13*

My own sight of the precious blood is for my comfort, but it is the Lord's sight of it that secures my safety. Even when I am unable to behold it, the Lord sees it and passes over me.

The Lord sees the deeper meaning, the infinite fullness of all that is meant by the death of His Son. He beheld Creation in its progress, and said, "It is very good"; but what does He say of redemption in its completeness? None can tell His delight in Jesus, His rest in the sweet savor which Jesus presented when He offered Himself without spot unto God.

Now rest we in calm security. We have God's Sacrifice and God's Word to create in us a sense of perfect security. He will pass over us, because He spared not our glorious Substitute. Justice joins hands with love to provide everlasting salvation for all the blood-besprinkled ones.

BLESSING IN THE CITY

Because you obey the voice of the LORD your God:
"Blessed shall you be in the city."

~ Deuteronomy 28:2-3

The city is full of noise and bustle: many are its temptations and worries. But to go there with the divine blessing takes off the edge of its difficulty, to remain there with that blessing is to find pleasure in its duties, and strength equal to its demands.

A blessing in the city may not make us great, but it will keep us good; it may also not make us rich, but it will preserve us honest. Whatever your job, the city will afford us opportunities for usefulness. We might prefer the quiet of a country life; but if called to town, we may certainly prefer it because there is room for our energies.

Today let us expect good things because of this promise, and let our prayer be to have an open ear to the voice of the Lord, and a ready hand to execute His bidding. There is great reward in keeping His commandments.

RETURN FROM BACKSLIDING

If you return to the Almighty,
you will be built up.

~ Job 22:23

Has sin pulled you down? Has the hand of the Lord gone out against you, so that you are broken in spirit? The first thing to do is return to the Lord.

With deep repentance and sincere faith, find your way back to Him. It is your duty, for you have turned away from Him whom you professed to serve. It is your wisdom, for you cannot strive against Him and prosper. It is your immediate necessity, for what He has done is nothing compared to what He may do in the way of chastisement.

See what a promise invites you! You shall be "built up." None but the Almighty can restore the tottering walls of your condition; but He can and He will do it if you return to Him. Do not delay. Hearty confession will ease you and humble faith will console you. Do this, and all will be well.

JOYFUL SECURITY

"I will uphold you with
My righteous right hand."

~ *Isaiah 41:10*

There are times when we feel that we must go down unless we have a very special support. Here we have it. God's right hand is a grand thing to lean upon. Mind, it is not only His hand, but His *right* hand: His power united with skill; His power where it is most dexterous.

This is not all, "I will uphold you with My *righteous* right hand." That hand, which He uses to maintain His holiness and to execute His royal sentences, shall be stretched out to hold up His trusting ones. The man whom God upholds, devils cannot throw down.

Weak may be our feet, but almighty is God's right hand. Rough may be the road, but Omnipotence is our upholding. We may boldly go forward. We shall not fall. God will not withdraw His strength, for His righteousness is there as well: He will be faithful to His promise.

THE DROSS PURGED

"I will bring the one-third through the fire,
will refine them as silver is refined, and test them
as gold is tested. They will call on My name,
and I will answer them. I will say,
'This is My people,' and each one will say,
'The LORD is my God.'"

~ Zechariah 13:9

Grace transmutes us into precious metal, and then the fire and the furnace follow as a necessary consequence. Would we sooner be accounted worthless that we might enjoy repose, like the stones of the field? No, Lord, we will gladly be cast into the furnace rather than be cast out from Your presence!

The fire only refines, it does not destroy. We are to be brought through the fire, not left in it. The Lord values His people as silver, and therefore He is at pains to purge away their dross. If we are wise, we will welcome the refining process.

O Lord, You test us indeed! We are ready to melt under the fierceness of the flame. Still, this is Your way and Your way is the best. Sustain us under the trial and complete the process of our purifying, and we will be Yours forever.

A Constant Witness

You will be His witness to all men of
what you have seen and heard.

~ Acts 22:15

Paul was chosen to see and hear the Lord speaking to him out of heaven, but it was meant to have an influence upon others too. It is to Paul that Europe owes the gospel.

The Lord has revealed to us to be witnesses, and it is at our peril that we hide the precious revelation. First, we must see and hear, or we shall have nothing to tell of our testimony. It must be personal; it must be for Christ; it must be constant and all absorbing; we are to be this above all other things, and to the exclusion of many other matters. Our witness must not be to a select few who will cheerfully receive us; but to "all men."

The text before us is a command and a promise, and we must not miss it – "You will be His witness." Lord, fulfill this word to me also!

ARE THE CHILDREN IN?

*"I will pour My Spirit on your descendants,
and My blessing on your offspring."*

~ Isaiah 44:3

Our dear children have not the Spirit of God by nature as we plainly see. We see much in them that makes us fear as to their future, and this drives us to agonizing prayer. This verse should greatly encourage us. It follows upon the words, "Fear not, O Jacob, My servant," and it may well banish our fears.

The Lord will give His Spirit; will give it plentifully, pouring it out; will give it effectively, so that it shall be a real and eternal blessing. Under this divine outpouring our children shall come forward and "one will say, 'I am the Lord's'; another will call himself by the name of Jacob."

This is one of those promises concerning which the Lord will be inquired of. Should we not pray for our offspring? The great Father takes pleasure in the prayers of fathers and mothers.

GOD DELIGHTS TO GIVE

*The Lord said to Abram, after Lot had separated
from him: "Lift your eyes now and look from the
place where you are – northward, southward,
eastward, and westward; for all the land which you
see I give to you and your descendants forever."*

~ Genesis 13:14-15

A special blessing for a memorable occasion. Abram
settled a family dispute, saying, "Let there be no
strife between you and me, for we are brethren,"
and hence he received the blessing which belongs to
peacemakers. The Lord and giver of peace delights
to manifest His grace to those who seek peace and
pursue it. If we desire closer communion with God,
we must keep closer to the ways of peace.

Abram behaved very generously to his kinsman,
giving him his choice of the land. If we deny ourselves for peace's sake, the Lord will more than make
it up to us. All things are ours. When we please the
Lord, He makes us to look everywhere and see all
things our own, whether things present, or things to
come. All are ours, and we are Christ's, and Christ
is God's.

BLESSED IN THE FIELD

Blessed shall you be in the country.

~ *Deuteronomy 28:3*

How often has the Lord met us when we have been alone! The hedges and the trees can bear witness to our joy. We look for such blessedness again.

We go to the field to labor as Adam did; and since the curse fell on the soil through the sin of Adam the first, it is a great comfort to find a blessing through Adam the second.

We go to the field for exercise, happy in the belief that the Lord will bless that exercise, and give us health, which we will use to His glory.

We go to the field to study nature, and there is nothing in knowledge of the visible creation that may not be sanctified to the highest uses by the divine benediction.

We have at last to go to the field to bury our dead; but remember; we are blessed, whether weeping at the tomb, or sleeping in it.

MERCY TO THE
UNDESERVING

He who trusts in the LORD,
mercy shall surround him.

~ Psalm 32:10

The truster above all men feels himself to be a sinner; yet, mercy is prepared for him. Lord, give me this mercy, even as I trust in You! Observe, my soul, what a bodyguard you have! Before and behind, and on all sides, ride these mounted guards of grace. We dwell in the center of the system of mercy, for we dwell in Christ Jesus.

My soul, what an atmosphere you breathe! As the air surrounds you, so does the mercy of the Lord. To the wicked there are many sorrows, but to you there are so many mercies that your sorrows are not worth mentioning.

David says, "Be glad in the LORD and rejoice, you righteous." In obedience to this precept my heart shall triumph in God, and I will tell of my gladness. As You have surrounded me with mercy, I will also surround Your altars, God, with songs of thanksgiving!

EVER MINDFUL

The LORD has been mindful of us;
He will bless us.

~ Psalm 115:12

I can set my seal to that first sentence. Yes, Jehovah has thought of us, provided for us, comforted us, delivered us, and guided us.

In all the movements of His providence He has been mindful of us, never overlooking us. His mind has been full of us – that is the other form of the word "mindful". This has been the case all along, without a single break.

The next sentence is a logical inference from the former one. Since God is unchangeable, He will continue to be mindful of us in the future, as He has been in the past; and His mindfulness is tantamount to blessing us.

The very indistinctness of the promise indicates its infinite reach. He will bless us after His own divine manner, and that forever and ever. Therefore, let us each say, "Bless the Lord, O my soul!"

YOU DEAL WITH GOD

"I will not execute the fierceness of My anger;
I will not again destroy Ephraim.
For I am God, and not man."

~ Hosea 11:9

The Lord thus makes known His sparing mercies. It may be that you are under heavy displeasure, and everything threatens your speedy doom. Let the text hold you up from despair. The Lord invites you to consider your ways and confess your sins. If He had been man, He would long ago have cut you off.

You rightly judge that He is angry, but He keeps not His anger forever: if you turn from sin to Jesus, God will turn from wrath. Because God is God, and not man, there is still forgiveness for you, even though you may be steeped up to your throat in iniquity.

No human being could have patience with you: you would have wearied out an angel, as you have wearied your sorrowing father, but the Father God is long-suffering. Come and try Him at once. Confess, believe, and turn from your evil way, and you shall be saved.

GOD CAN MAKE YOU STRONG

*"Be strong and do not let your hands be weak,
for your work shall be rewarded!"*

~ 2 Chronicles 15:7

God did great things for King Asa and Judah, yet they were a feeble folk. Their feet were tottering in the ways of the Lord, and their hearts hesitating, so that they had to be warned that the Lord would be with them, but if they forsook Him He would leave them. The Lord's design was to confirm them in His way, and make them strong in righteousness. So ought it to be with us. God deserves to be served with all the energy of which we are capable.

If the service of God is worth anything, it is worth everything. We shall find our best reward in the Lord's work if we do it with determined diligence.

Our labor is not in vain in the Lord, and we know it. Half-hearted work will bring no reward, but when we throw our whole soul into the cause, we shall see prosperity.

GOD WILL ANSWER

He will fulfill the desire of whose who fear Him;
He also will hear their cry and save them.

~ *Psalm 145:19*

The Father's own Spirit has wrought this desire in us, and therefore He will answer our cry. Those who fear Him are men under the holiest influence and, therefore, their desire is to glorify God, and enjoy Him forever. Like Daniel, they are men of desires, and the Lord God will cause them to realize their aspirations.

God-fearing men desire to be holy, useful, and a blessing to others, so as to honor their Lord. They desire supplies for their need, help under burdens, guidance in perplexity, deliverance in distress; and sometimes this desire is so strong, and their case so pressing, that they cry out in agony, and then the Lord does all that is needful according to this Word and saves them.

Yes, if we fear God, we have nothing else to fear; if we cry to the Lord, our salvation is certain.

BETTER FARTHER ON

"Though I have afflicted you,
I will afflict you no more."

~ *Nahum 1:12*

There is a limit to affliction. God sends it and God removes it. Remember that our grief will surely and finally end when this earthly life is over. Let us quietly wait, and patiently endure the will of the Lord till He comes.

Meanwhile, our Father in heaven takes away the rod when His design in using it is fully served. Or, if the affliction is sent for testing us, that our graces may glorify God, it will end when the Lord has made us bear witness to His praise.

There may even today be "a great calm." We may, before many hours are past, be just as happy as now we are sorrowful. It is not hard for the Lord to turn night into day. He who sends the clouds can just as easily clear the skies. Let us be of good cheer. Let us sing Hallelujah in anticipation.

CONTINUAL GUIDANCE

The LORD will guide you continually.

~ Isaiah 58:11

Have you lost your way? Are you entangled in a dark wood, unable to find your path? Stand still, and see the salvation of God. He knows the way, and He will direct you if you cry unto Him.

Every day brings its own perplexity. How sweet to feel that the guidance of the Lord is continual! If we abstain from self-will, He will direct every step of our road, every hour of the day, every day of the year, every year of our lives.

But this promise is only for those who extend their souls to the hungry (v. 10). If we show a tender care for our fellow man, then will the Lord attend to our necessities and make Himself our continual Guide. Jesus is the Leader not of misers, but of the kind and tenderhearted. Such persons are pilgrims who shall never miss their way.

BLESSING ON LITTLENESS

He will bless those who fear the LORD,
both small and great.

~ *Psalm 115:13*

This is a word of cheer to those who are of humble station. God cares for the small things in creation, and even regards sparrows in their lighting upon the ground. Nothing is small to God, for He makes use of insignificant agents for the accomplishment of His purposes.

Among those who fear the Lord there are little and great. Some are babes, and others are giants. But all are blessed. Little faith is blessed faith. Trembling hope is blessed hope. Every grace of the Holy Spirit, even though it be only in the bud, bears a blessing within it.

Moreover, the Lord Jesus bought both the small and the great with the same precious blood, and He has engaged to preserve the lambs as well as the full-grown sheep. No mother overlooks her child because it is little; the smaller it is, the more tenderly does she nurse it.

PAST DELIVERANCE
ENCOURAGES FAITH

David said, "The LORD who delivered me from
the paw of the lion and from the paw of the bear,
He will deliver me from the hand of this Philistine."

~ 1 Samuel 17:37

This is not a promise if we consider only the words, but it is truly so as to its sense; for David spoke a word, which the Lord endorsed by making true. He argued from past deliverances that he should receive help in a new danger. The Lord's former dealings with His believing people will be repeated.

Come, then, let us recall the Lord's former loving-kindnesses. Will He not again save us? We are sure He will. As David ran to meet his foe, so will we. The Lord has been with us, He is with us, and He has said, "I will never leave you, nor forsake you." Why do we tremble?

God is the same, and His honor is as much concerned in the one case as in the other. He did not save us from the beasts of the forest to let a giant kill us. Let us be of good courage.

UNBROKEN FELLOWSHIP
IS ESSENTIAL

"If you abide in Me, and My words abide in you,
you will ask what you desire,
and it shall be done for you."

~ *John 15:7*

To abide in Jesus is never to quit Him for another love, but to remain in living, loving, conscious union with Him. The branch is not only ever near the stem, but ever receiving life and fruitfulness from it.

"Ask what you desire" is for Enochs who walk with God, for Johns who lie in the Lord's bosom, for those whose union with Christ leads to constant communion.

The heart must remain in love, the mind must be rooted in faith, the hope must be cemented to the Word, the whole man must be joined unto the Lord.

Carte blanche can only be given to one whose very life is, "Not I, but Christ lives in me." You who break your fellowship, what power you lose! If you would be mighty in your pleadings, the Lord Himself must abide in you, and you in Him.

HEAR SO AS TO BE HEARD

"If you abide in Me, and My words abide in you,
you will ask what you desire,
and it shall be done for you."

~ *John 15:7*

Note that we must hear Jesus speak if we expect Him to hear us speak. If we have no ear for Christ, He will have no ear for us.

Moreover, what is heard must remain; it must live in us, it must abide in our character as a force and a power.

If our Lord's words are received and abide in us, what a boundless field of privilege is opened up to us! We are to have our will in prayer, because we have already surrendered our will to the Lord's command. Thus are Elijahs trained to handle the keys of heaven, and lock or loose the clouds.

Do we humbly desire to be intercessors for the church and the world, and desire to be able to have what we desire of the Lord? Then we must bow our ear to His voice and treasure up His words and carefully obey them.

SET APART

"You shall be named the priests of the LORD."

~ *Isaiah 61:6*

This literal promise to Israel belongs spiritually to the seed after the Spirit, namely, to all believers. If we live up to our privileges, we shall live unto God so clearly and distinctly, that men shall see that we are set apart for holy service and shall name us the priests of the Lord. We may work or trade, as others do, and yet we may be solely and wholly the ministering servants of God.

This being our one aim, we may leave distracting concerns to those who have no higher calling. They may manage politics, puzzle out financial problems, and discuss science; but we will give ourselves unto such service as becomes those who, like the Lord Jesus, are ordained to a perpetual priesthood.

Accepting this honorable promise as involving a sacred duty, let us put on the vestments of holiness, and minister before the Lord all day long.

TRUTH ESTABLISHED

The truthful lip shall be established forever,
but a lying tongue is but for a moment.

~ Proverbs 12:19

Truth wears well. Time tests it, but it endures. If, then, I have spoken the truth, and have for the present to suffer for it, I must be content to wait. If I believe the truth of God and declare it, I may meet with much opposition, but I need not fear, for ultimately the truth must prevail.

The triumph of falsehood is temporary. "A lying tongue is but for a moment" (v. 19). On the other hand, how worthy of an immortal being is the defense of that truth which can never change; the everlasting gospel, which is established in the immutable truth of an unchanging God! He who speaks the truth of God will put to shame all the devils in hell.

Ensure you're on the side of truth in all things, both in small things and great; but especially on the side of Him by whom grace and truth have come among men!

STEADFAST TRUSTFULNESS

He will not be afraid of evil tidings;
his heart is steadfast, trusting in the LORD.

~ Psalm 112:7

Suspense is dreadful, and when we have no news from home we often grow anxious. Faith is the cure for this condition: the Lord, by His Spirit, settles the mind in holy serenity, and all fear is gone for the future and the present.

The steadfastness of heart spoken of by the psalmist must be diligently sought after. It is the general condition of unwavering trustfulness in God, the confidence that we have in Him that He will neither do us ill, nor suffer anyone else to harm us.

Let the morrow be what it may, our God is the God of tomorrow. Whatever events may have happened, which to us are unknown, our Jehovah is God of the unknown as well as of the known. We are determined to trust the Lord, come what may. If the very worst should happen, our God is still the greatest and best. Therefore will we not fear.

REAL ESTATE IN HEAVEN

… Knowing that you have a better and
an enduring possession for yourselves in heaven.

~ Hebrews 10:34

Our substance here is very unsubstantial. But God has given us a promise of real estate in the glory-land, and that promise comes to our hearts with such certainty that we know in ourselves that we have an enduring substance there. Yes, we have it even now. We have the title deed of heaven, we have the earnest of it, we have the first fruits of it. We have heaven in price, in promise, and in principle.

Should not that thought console you in present losses? Our finances we may lose, but our treasure is safe; for our Savior lives, and the place that He has prepared for us abides.

There is a better land, a better substance, a better promise; and all this comes to us by a better covenant. So let us be in better spirits, and say unto the Lord, "Every day will I bless You; and praise Your name forever."

WHAT FOLLOWS US

*Surely goodness and mercy shall
follow me all the days of my life.*

~ *Psalm 23:6*

A devout poet sings:

> Lord, when Thou
> Puttest in my time a day,
> as Thou dost now
> Unknown in other years, grant, I entreat,
> Such grace illumine it, that whatever its phase
> It add to holiness, and lengthen praise!

This day comes but once in four years. Goodness and mercy, like two guards, have followed us from day to day, and as this out-of-the-way day is one of the days of our lives, the two guardian angels will be with us today also.

Goodness to supply our needs, and mercy to blot out our sins – these shall attend our every step this day and every day till days shall be no more. By inventiveness of love let us make this twenty-ninth of February a day to be remembered forever.

March

JOY FOR THE CAST OUT

*"Hear the word of the LORD, you who tremble
at His word: 'Your brethren who hated you,
who cast you out for My name's sake, said,
"Let the LORD be glorified, that we may see
your joy." But they shall be ashamed.'"*

~ Isaiah 66:5

Possibly this verse may not apply to one in a thousand of readers, but the Lord cheers that one in such words as these. Let us pray for all who are cast out wrongfully from the society that they love. May the Lord appear to their joy!

The text applies to truly gracious men who were cast out because of their fidelity and their holiness. This must have been very bitter to them, especially because their casting out was done in the name of religion and professedly with the view of glorifying God. How much is done for the devil in the name of God!

The appearing of the Lord for them is the hope of His persecuted people. He appears as the advocate and defender of His elect, and when He does so, it means a clear deliverance for the God-fearing, and shame for their oppressors. Lord, fulfill this word!

GIVING WITHOUT A WHISPER

*"When you do a charitable deed, do not let your
left hand know what your right hand is doing,
that your charitable deed may be in secret;
and your Father who sees in secret
will Himself reward you openly."*

~ *Matthew 6:3-4*

Let us hide away our charity, yes, hide it even from ourselves. Give so often and so much as a matter of course that you no more take note that you have helped the poor than that you have eaten your regular meals. Do your alms without even whispering to yourself, "How generous I am!" Do not attempt to reward yourself so. Leave the matter with God, who never fails to see, to record, and to reward.

Blessed is the man who is busy in secret with his kindness: he finds a special joy in His unknown benevolences. This is the bread which, eaten by stealth, is sweeter than the banquets of kings. How can I indulge myself today with this delightful luxury?

The Lord Himself will personally see to the rewarding of the secret giver of alms. This will be in His own way and time, and He will choose the very best.

NOT LEFT TO PERISH

You will not leave my soul in Sheol, nor will You allow Your Holy One to see corruption.

~ *Psalm 16:10*

This word has its proper fulfillment in the Lord Jesus; but it applies also, with a variation, to all who are in Him. The general meaning, rather than the specific application, is that to which we would call our readers' thoughts.

We may descend very low in spirit till we seem to be plunged in the abyss of hell, but we shall not be left there. We may appear to be at death's door in heart and soul, but we cannot remain there. We may go very low; we may stay in the lowest dungeon of doubt for a while, but we shall not perish there.

The star of hope is still in the sky when the night is blackest. The Lord will not forget us and hand us over to the enemy. Let us rest in hope. Out of death, and darkness, and despair we shall yet arise to life, light, and liberty.

HONOR GOD

"Those who honor Me I will honor."

~ *1 Samuel 2:30*

Do I make the honor of God the great object of my life and the rule of my conduct? If so, He will honor me. I may not receive honor from man, but God will Himself put honor upon me.

Eli did not honor the Lord by ruling his household well, and his sons had not honored the Lord by their behavior. Therefore the Lord did not honor them, but took the high priesthood out of their family and made young Samuel to be ruler instead of any of their line.

If I would have my family ennobled, I must honor the Lord in all things. God may allow the wicked to win worldly honors, but the dignity, glory and honor which He Himself gives, He reserves for those who take care to honor Him.

Let me think what I can do this day to honor the Lord, since He will honor me.

HOME BLESSINGS

He blesses the home of the just.

~ *Proverbs 3:33*

He fears the Lord, and therefore he comes under His divine protection. His home is an abode of love, a school of holy training, and a place of heavenly light. Therefore the Lord blesses his habitation. It may be a humble cottage or a lordly mansion; but the Lord's blessing comes because of the character of the inhabitant, not because of the size of the dwelling.

That house is most blessed where the master and mistress are God-fearing people; but a son or daughter or even a servant may bring a blessing on a whole household.

The Lord often preserves; prospers, and provides for a family for the sake of one or two in it who are "just" persons in His esteem, because His grace has made them so. Let us have Jesus for our constant guest and then we shall be blessed indeed.

GUARDIAN OF
THE FATHERLESS

"In You the fatherless finds mercy."

~ Hosea 14:3

This is an excellent reason for casting away all other confidences and relying upon the Lord alone. When a child is orphaned, or a man loses every object of dependence, he may cast himself upon the living God and find in Him all that he needs.

Some children who have fathers are not much better off because of them, but the fatherless with God are rich. Better to have God and no other friend than all the patrons on the earth and no God. So long as the Lord remains the fountain of mercy to us, we are not truly orphaned.

Let fatherless children plead the gracious word for this morning, and let all who have been bereaved of visible support do the same. Lord, let me find mercy in You! The more needy and helpless I am, the more confidently do I appeal to Your loving heart.

FROM FETTERS FREE

The LORD gives freedom to the prisoners.

~ *Psalm 146:7*

The Lord has done it. Remember Joseph, Jeremiah, Peter, and many others. He can do it still. He breaks the bars of brass with a word, and snaps the fetters of iron with a look. He is doing it. At this moment doors are flying back and fetters are dropping to the ground.

He will delight to set you free if you are mourning because of sorrow, doubt, and fear. It will be a joy to Jesus to give you liberty. Only trust Him, and He will be your Emancipator.

Believe in Him in spite of the stone walls, or the manacles of iron. Satan cannot hold you, sin cannot enchain you, even despair cannot bind you, if you believe in the Lord, in the freeness of His grace, and the fullness of His power to save.

Defy the enemy, and let the word now before you be your song of deliverance: "Jehovah frees the prisoners."

OUR SUBSTANCE BLESSED

*Blessed shall be your basket
and your kneading bowl.*

~ Deuteronomy 28:5

Obedience brings a blessing on all the provisions that our industry earns for us. Perhaps ours is a hand-basket portion. If we live from hand to mouth, getting each day's supply in the day, we are as well off as Israel; for the Lord only gave them a day's manna at a time. What more did *they* need? What more do *we* need?

But if we have a store, how much we need the Lord to bless it! For there is the care of getting, of keeping, of managing, of using, and, unless the Lord bless it, these cares will rule us.

O Lord, bless our substance. Enable us to use it for Your glory. Help us to keep worldly things in their proper places, and never may our savings endanger the saving of our souls.

PRAYER FOR PEACE

"Seek the peace of the city where I have caused you to be carried away captive, and pray to the LORD for it; for in its peace you will have peace."

~ *Jeremiah 29:7*

The principle involved in this text would suggest to all of us who are the Lord's strangers and foreigners that we should be desirous to promote the peace and prosperity of the people among whom we dwell. Our nation and our city especially should be blessed by our constant intercession.

Eagerly let us pray for peace, both at home and abroad. If strife should cause bloodshed in our streets, or if foreign battle should slay our brave soldiers, we should all bewail the calamity; let us therefore pray for peace and diligently promote those principles by which the classes at home and the races abroad may be bound together in bonds of harmony.

Today let us be much in prayer for our country, confessing national sins, and asking for national pardon and blessing, for Jesus' sake.

WALK IN LIGHT

"I have come as a light into the world, that whoever believes in Me should not abide in darkness."

~ John 12:46

This world is dark as midnight; Jesus came so that we may have light and may no longer sit in the gloom that covers mankind.

If we trust in Jesus we shall enter into the warm light of a day that shall never end. Why do we not come out into the light at once?

A cloud may sometimes hover over us, but we shall not abide in darkness if we believe in Jesus. He has come to give us daylight. If we have faith, we have the privilege of sunlight: let us enjoy it. From the night of ignorance, doubt, despair, sin, and dread, Jesus has come to set us free.

Shake off your depression and abide in the light. In Jesus is your hope, your joy, your heaven. Look to Him only, and you will rejoice as the birds rejoice at sunrise, and as the angels rejoice before the throne.

WHOSE BATTLE?

*Then all this assembly shall know that the LORD
does not save with sword and spear; for the battle
is the LORD's, and He will give you into our hands.*

~ 1 Samuel 17:47

The battle is the Lord's and we may be certain of victory. The Lord is too much forgotten by men and when there is an opportunity to make men see that God can achieve His purposes without man, it is a priceless occasion. In this verse it is a grand thing for David to have no sword, and yet for him to know that his God will overthrow a whole army.

If we are contending for truth and righteousness, do not tarry till we have talent or wealth, or any other form of visible power at our disposal; but with the stones we find in the brook, and with our sling, let us run to meet the enemy.

If it were our own battle, we might not be confident; but if we are standing up for Jesus, and warring in His strength alone, let us have no trace of hesitancy, for who can withstand us?

GOING OUT WITH JOY

And of Zebulun he said:
"Rejoice, Zebulun, in your going out."

~ Deuteronomy 33:18

The blessings of the tribes are ours, for we are the true Israel who worship God in the spirit, and have no confidence in the flesh. When we go out, we will look out for occasions of joy.

When we travel, the providence of God is our convoy. When we emigrate, the Lord is with us on land and sea. When we go out as missionaries, Jesus says, "I am with you always." When we go out to our labor, we may do so with pleasure, for God will be with us from morn till eve.

Fear sometimes creeps over us for the unknown, but this blessing may serve as a word of good cheer. As we pack up for moving, let us drop this verse into our hearts and keep it there, let us lay it on our tongue to make us sing. Let us, in our every movement, praise the Lord with joyful hearts.

DESPISE NOT YOUR YOUTH

Then said I: "Ah, Lord GOD! Behold, I cannot speak,
for I am a youth." But the LORD said to me:
"Do not say, 'I am a youth,' for you shall go
to all to whom I send you, and whatever
I command you, you shall speak."

~ Jeremiah 1:6-7

Jeremiah was young and felt a natural shrinking when sent upon a great errand by the Lord; but He who sent him would not have him say, "I am a youth." What Jeremiah was in himself must be lost in the consideration that he was chosen to speak for God, and he would be enabled to do so in strength not his own.

God knows how young you are, and how slender your knowledge and experience; but if He chooses to send you somewhere, it is not for you to shrink from the heavenly call. God will magnify Himself in our feebleness. If you were as old as Methuselah, how much would your years help you? If you were as wise as Solomon, you might be equally as willful as he. Keep to your message and it will be your wisdom; follow your marching orders and they will be your discretion.

TENDER COMFORT

"As one whom his mother comforts,
so I will comfort you."

~ *Isaiah 66:13*

A mother's comfort! This is tenderness itself. A child can tell her all, and she will sympathize as nobody else can. Of all comforters, the child loves best his own mother.

Does Jehovah condescend to act the mother's part? This is goodness indeed. We readily perceive Him as a father, but as a mother also? Does not this invite us to unreserved confidence, to sacred rest? When God Himself becomes "the Comforter," no anguish can long abide. Let us tell our trouble, even though sobs and sighs should become our readiest utterance. He will not despise us for our tears – our mother did not.

He will consider our weakness as she did, and He will put away our faults, only in a surer, safer way than our mother could do. Let us begin the day with our loving God and finish it in the same company, since mothers weary not of their children.

GOD IS A SANCTUARY

Thus says the Lord GOD: "Although I have cast them
far off among the Gentiles, and although
I have scattered them among the countries,
yet I shall be a little sanctuary for them
in the countries where they have gone."

~ Ezekiel 11:16

Banished from the public means of grace, we are not removed from the grace of the means. The Lord who places His people where they feel as exiles will Himself be with them, and be to them all that they could have had at home.

God is to His people a place of *refuge*. They find sanctuary with Him from every adversary. He is their place of *worship* too. He is with them as with Jacob when he slept in the open field, and rising, said, "Surely God was in this place." To them also He will be a sanctuary of *quiet*, like the Holy of Holies, which was the noiseless abode of the Eternal.

God Himself, in Christ Jesus, is the sanctuary of *mercy*. In God we find the shrine of *holiness* and of *communion*. What more do we need? Lord, fulfill this promise and be ever to us as a little sanctuary!

TO OTHERS, AN "ENSAMPLE"

The things which you learned and
received and heard and saw in me,
these do, and the God of peace will be with you.

~ Philippians 4:9

Oh, for grace to imitate Paul this day and every day!

If we carry into practice the Pauline teaching, we may claim the promise which is now open before us; and what a promise it is! God, who loves peace, makes peace, and breathes peace, will be with us. Thus we have the fountain as well as the streams, the sun as well as its beams.

If the God of peace be with us, we shall enjoy the peace of God, which passes all understanding, even though outward circumstances should threaten to disturb us.

It is in the way of truth that real peace is found. If we quit the faith or leave the path of righteousness under the notion of promoting peace, we shall be greatly mistaken. Let us keep to Paul's line, and we shall have the God of peace with us as He was with the apostle.

FEAR TO FEAR

"Do not be afraid of their faces,
for I am with you to deliver you," says the LORD.

~ *Jeremiah 1:8*

Whenever fear comes in and makes us falter, we are in danger of falling into sin. Yet what a reason for bravery is here! God is with those who are with Him. God will never be away when the hour of struggle comes. Do they threaten you? Who are you that you should be afraid of a man? Your God will find bread and water for His servants. Can you not trust Him? Do they pour ridicule upon you? Bear it for Christ's sake and even rejoice because of it.

God is with the true and the just to deliver them, and He will deliver you. Remember how Daniel came out of the lions' den and the three holy children out of the furnace. The Lord will bear you through anything and make you more than a conqueror. Fear to fear. Be afraid to be afraid. Rise up, saying, "I will trust, and not be afraid."

CONTINUE UPRIGHT

The prayer of the upright is His delight.

~ *Proverbs 15:8*

God takes great pleasure in the prayers of upright men; He even calls them His delight. Our first concern is to be upright, with integrity. If we try crooked ways our prayers will be shut out of heaven.

Are we following the Lord's revealed will? Then let us pray much and pray in faith. If our prayer is God's delight, let us not stint Him in that which gives Him pleasure.

He does not consider the grammar of it, the metaphysics of it, or the rhetoric of it; in all these, men might despise it. Yet, He, as a Father, takes pleasure in the lispings of His own babes, the stammerings of His newborn sons and daughters.

Should we not delight in prayer since the Lord delights in it? Let us make errands to the throne. The Lord finds us enough reasons for prayer, and we ought to thank Him that it is so.

March 19

BECOMING FIT FOR GLORY

The LORD will give grace and glory.

~ Psalm 84:11

Today we shall freely receive sustaining, strengthening, sanctifying, satisfying grace. God has given daily grace until now; and as for the future, that grace is still sufficient. He gives liberally and without reproach.

The Lord may not give gold, but He will give grace: He may not give gain, but He will give grace. He will certainly send us trial, but He will give grace in proportion thereto. We may be called to labor and to suffer, but with the call there will come all the grace required.

What an "and" is that in the text: "and glory!" We do not need glory yet; but we shall have it in time. After we have eaten the bread of grace, we shall drink the wine of glory. These words "and glory" are enough to make a man dance for joy. A little while, a little while, and then glory forever!

DIVINE PROVISION

"Now if God so clothes the grass of the field,
which today is, and tomorrow is thrown into the oven,
will He not much more clothe you, O you of little faith?"

~ *Matthew 6:30*

Clothes are expensive, and poor believers may be led into anxiety as to where their next suit will come from. Our heavenly Father clothes the grass of the field with splendor: will He not clothe His own children? We are sure He will. There may be many a patch and a darn, but clothing we shall have.

A poor minister found his clothes nearly threadbare and so far gone that they would hardly hold together; but as a servant of the Lord, he expected his Master to find him his livery. It so happened that on a visit to a friend, I had the loan of the good man's pulpit, and it came into my mind to make a collection for him, and *there was his suit*.

The Lord, who made man so that when he had sinned he needed garments, also in mercy supplied him with them.

AVOID THAT SLIP

Then you will walk safely in your way,
and your foot will not stumble.

~ Proverbs 3:23

If we follow the ways of wisdom and holiness, we shall be preserved in them. There is a way for every man, and if we devoutly walk therein in the fear of God, He will preserve us from evil. We may not travel luxuriously, but we shall walk safely.

Our greatest danger lies in ourselves: our feeble foot is sadly apt to stumble. Let us ask for more moral strength, that our tendency to slip may be overcome. Some stumble because they do not see the stone in the way: divine grace enables us to perceive sin and so to avoid it. Let us plead this promise and trust in Him who upholds His chosen.

Oh, for grace to walk this day without a single stumble! Our cry should be that we may not make the smallest slip with our feet, but may at the last adore Him who is able to keep us from stumbling.

GRACE FOR THE HUMBLE

"God gives grace to the humble."

~ James 4:6

Humble hearts seek grace, and therefore they get it. They are grateful for grace and give the Lord the glory of it, and hence it is consistent with His honor to give it to them.

Come, take a lowly place. Be little in your own esteem, that the Lord may make much of you. Some are proud of being humble, and this is one of the very worst sorts of pride.

We are needy, helpless, undeserving, creatures; and if we are not humble, we ought to be. Let us humble ourselves because of our sins against humility, and then the Lord will give us to taste of His favor. It is grace that makes us humble, and grace that finds in this humility an opportunity for pouring in more grace. Let us go down that we may rise. Let us be poor in spirit that God may make us rich.

A SURE GUIDE

*"I will bring the blind by a way
they did not know."*

~ *Isaiah 42:16*

Think of the infinitely glorious Jehovah acting as a Guide to the blind! A blind man cannot find a way he does not know; even when he knows the road, it is hard for him to traverse it.

As to the future, all of us are blind, but the Lord Jesus will lead us even to our journey's end. We cannot guess how deliverance will come to us, but the Lord knows, and He will lead us till we have escaped every danger.

Happy are those who place their hand in that of the Great Guide. He will bring them all the way; and when He has brought them home to glory and has opened their eyes to see the way by which He has led them, what a song of gratitude will they sing unto God! Lord, lead Your poor blind child this day, for I know not my way!

ESTABLISHED AND KEPT

*The Lord is faithful, who will establish
you and guard you from the evil one.*

~ 2 Thessalonians 3:3

Men are often as devoid of reason as of faith. There is no use in arguing with them or trying to be at peace with them: they are false at heart and deceitful in speech. Shall we worry ourselves with them? No, let us turn to the Lord, for He is faithful. No promise from His Word will ever be broken. He is neither unreasonable in His demands upon us, nor unfaithful to our claims upon Him.

He will establish us so that wicked men shall not cause our downfall. What a blessing for us that we need not contend with men, but are allowed to shelter ourselves in the Lord Jesus.

There is one true heart, one faithful mind, one unchanging Love; there let us repose. The Lord will fulfill the purpose of His grace to us His servants, and we need not allow a shadow of a fear to fall upon our spirits.

REFRESHING SLEEP

When you lie down, you will not be afraid;
yes, you will lie down and your sleep will be sweet.

~ Proverbs 3:24

When we go to bed at night, let this word smooth our pillow. We cannot guard ourselves in sleep, but the Lord will keep us through the night.

If, with our lying down, there is a laying down of all cares and ambitions, we shall get refreshment out of our beds such as the anxious and covetous never find in theirs. Ill dreams shall be banished, or even if they come, we shall wipe out the impression of them, knowing that they are only dreams.

If we sleep thus we shall do well. How sweetly Peter slept when even the angel's light did not wake him, and he needed a hard jog in the side to wake him up. And yet he was sentenced to die on the morrow. "He gives His beloved sleep."

To have sweet sleep we must have sweet lives, sweet tempers, sweet meditations, and sweet love.

THE CARE OF THE POOR

*The LORD will strengthen him
on his bed of illness.*

~ *Psalm 41:3*

Remember that this is a promise to the man who considers the poor. Are you one of these?

See how in the hour of sickness the God of the poor will bless the man who cares for the poor! The everlasting arms shall stay up his soul, as friendly hands and downy pillows stay up the body of the sick. How tender and sympathizing is this image; how near it brings our God to our infirmities and sicknesses!

Grace is the best of restoratives; divine love is the safest stimulant for a languishing patient, it makes the soul strong as a giant, even when the bones are breaking through the skin. There is no physician like the Lord, no tonic like His promise, no wine like His love.

If the reader has failed in his duty to the poor, let him see what he is losing, and at once become their friend and helper.

COME NEAR TO GOD

Draw near to God and
He will draw near to you.

~ James 4:8

The nearer we come to God, the more graciously will He reveal Himself to us. When the prodigal returns, his father runs to meet him. When the wandering dove comes back, Noah puts out his hand to pull her in to him. Come then, let us draw near to God who so graciously awaits us, who comes to meet us.

In Isaiah 58:9 the Lord seems to put Himself at the disposal of His people, saying to them, "Here I am," as much as to say, "What can I do for you? I am waiting to bless you." How can we hesitate to draw near? God is near to forgive, to bless, to comfort, to help.

Let us aim to get near to God. This done, all is done. If we seek the Lord alone, He will continue to come nearer and yet nearer to us by fuller and more joyful fellowship.

LEAD THE WAY

*The LORD will make you
the head and not the tail.*

~ Deuteronomy 28:13

If we obey the Lord, He will compel our adversaries to see that His blessing rests upon us.

It is for saints to lead the way among men: they are not to be the tail, to be dragged hither and thither by others. We must not yield to the spirit of the age, but compel the age to do homage to Christ.

Has not the Lord Jesus made His people priests? Are we not in Christ made kings to reign upon the earth? How, then, can we be the servants of custom, the slaves of human opinion?

Have you taken up your true position for Jesus? Too many are silent. Should we allow the name of the Lord Jesus to be kept in the background? Should not our religion lead the way and be the ruling force with ourselves and others?

DAUNTLESS FAITH

*"I am with you, and no one will
attack you to hurt you."*

~ *Acts 18:10*

So long as the Lord God had work for Paul to do in Corinth, the fury of the mob was restrained. The Jews opposed themselves and blasphemed; but they could not stop the preaching of the gospel, or the conversion of the hearers. God has power over the most violent minds. "By the power of Your arm they will be as still as a stone – until Your people pass by, O LORD" (Exod. 15:16).

Do not, therefore, feel any fear of man when you know that you are doing your duty. Go straight on, as Jesus would have done, and those who oppose shall be as a bruised reed.

A dauntless faith in God brushes fear aside like cobwebs in a giant's path. He who makes the devil flee at a word, can certainly control the devil's agents. Therefore, go forward, and where you looked to meet with foes you will find friends.

PRAYER, THANKSGIVING, PRAISE

Be anxious for nothing, but in everything by prayer
and supplication, with thanksgiving, let your requests
be made known to God; and the peace of God,
which surpasses all understanding, will guard
your hearts and minds through Christ Jesus.

~ Philippians 4:6-7

No care, but all prayer. No anxiety, but joyful communion with God. Carry your desires to the Lord of your life, the guardian of your soul. Go to Him with two portions of prayer and one of fragrant praise. Do not pray doubtfully, but thankfully. Hide nothing. Allow no want to lie rankling in your bosom; make known your requests. Run not to man. Go only to your God, who loves you.

This shall bring you God's own peace. It will enfold you in its infinite embrace. Heart and mind through Christ Jesus shall be steeped in a sea of rest.

Come life or death, poverty, pain, slander, you shall dwell in Jesus above every ruffling wind or darkening cloud. Will you not obey this dear command?

PRESENCE OF MIND

Do not be afraid of sudden terror, nor of trouble from the wicked when it comes; for the LORD will be your confidence, and will keep your foot from being caught.

~ Proverbs 3:25-26

God would have His people manifest *courage*. Since the Lord Himself may suddenly come, we ought not to be surprised at anything sudden. Serenity under the rush and roar of unexpected evils is a precious gift of divine love.

The Lord would have His chosen display *discrimination*, so that they may see that the desolation of the wicked is not a real calamity to the universe. Sin alone is evil; the punishment that follows is as a preserving salt to keep society from putrefying. We should be far more shocked at the sin that deserves hell, than at the hell that comes out of sin.

So, too, should the Lord's people exhibit great *quietness of spirit*. Satan and his serpent seed are full of all subtlety; but those who walk with God shall not be taken in their deceitful snares. Go on, believer in Jesus, and let the Lord be Your confidence.

April

THE KING'S HIGHWAY

*Whoever walks the road, although
a fool, shall not go astray.*

~ Isaiah 35:8

The way of holiness is so straight and plain that the simplest minds cannot go astray if they constantly follow it. The worldly wise have many twists and turns; they make terrible blunders and generally miss their end.

When men choose worldly policy as their road, it leads them over dark mountains. Gracious minds know no better than to do as the Lord bids them; this keeps them in the king's highway, and under royal protection.

Never attempt to help yourself out of a difficulty by a falsehood or by a questionable act; but keep in the middle of the high road of truth and integrity, and you will be following the best possible course. Be just and fear not. God's way must be the best way. Follow it though men think you a fool, and you will be truly wise.

TRUE HEART ENERGY

*Meditate on these things; give yourself entirely to them,
that your progress may be evident to all.*

~ *1 Timothy 4:15*

This is a promise that, by diligent meditation and the giving up of our whole mind to our work for the Lord, we shall make a progress which all can see.

Not by hasty reading, but by deep meditation, we profit by the Word of God. Not by doing a great deal of work in a slovenly manner, but by giving our best thought to what we attempt, we shall get real profit. "In all *labor* there is profit" (Prov. 14:23), but not in fuss and hurry, without true heart energy.

Am I a minister? Let me be a minister wholly, and not spend my energies upon secondary concerns. Am I a Christian? Let me make my service of Jesus my occupation, my life's work, my one pursuit.

We must be in-and-in with Jesus, and then out-and-out for Jesus, or else we shall make neither progress nor profit.

SENSITIVE TO WARNING

*"Because your heart was tender, and you humbled
yourself before the LORD when you heard what I
spoke against this place and against its inhabitants,
that they would become a desolation and
a curse, and you tore your clothes and wept
before Me, I also have heard you," says the LORD.*

~ 2 Kings 22:19

Many despise warnings and perish: Happy is he who trembles at the word of God. Josiah did so, and he was spared of evil, which the Lord determined to send upon Judah because of her great sins. Have you this tenderness? Then you also shall be spared in the evil day.

God sets a mark upon the men that sigh and cry because of the sin of the times. The destroying angel is commanded to keep his sword in its sheath till the elect of God are sheltered. Are the times threatening? Do you dread national chastisement upon this polluted nation? Well you may rest in this promise, "You shall be gathered to your grave in peace; and your eyes shall not see all the calamity which I will bring on this place" (2 Kings 22:20).

GOD'S HORNETS

*"I will send hornets before you,
which shall drive out the Hivite, the Canaanite,
and the Hittite from before you."*

~ Exodus 23:28

What the hornets were we need not consider. They were God's own army, which He sent before His people to sting their enemies and render Israel's conquest easy. Our God, by His own chosen means, will fight for His people before they come into the actual battle.

Let us never fear. Oftentimes when we march to the conflict, we find no host to contend with. "The LORD will fight for you, and you shall hold your peace" (Exod. 14:14). We could never dream of the victory being won by such means as Jehovah will use. We must obey our marching orders and go forth to the conquest of the nations for Jesus, and we shall find that the Lord has prepared the way for us, so that in the end we shall joyfully confess, "His own right hand and His holy arm, have gotten him the victory."

NOT FORGOTTEN

*"You are My servant; O Israel,
you will not be forgotten by Me!"*

~ Isaiah 44:21

Our Jehovah cannot so forget His servants as to cease to love them. He chose them not for a time, but forever. He knew what they would be when He called them into the divine family. He blots out their sins like a cloud; and we may be sure that He will not turn them away for iniquities that He has blotted out.

He will not forget them so as to cease to think of them. Men forget us: we have no abiding place in the fickle hearts of men, but God will never forget one of His true servants. We have been loved too long and bought at too great a price to be forgotten.

Jesus sees in us His soul's travail, and that He never can forget. The Lord thinks on us. This day we shall be assisted and sustained. Oh, that the Lord may never be forgotten by us!

ONE KING, ONE LORD

And the LORD shall be King over all the earth.
In that day it shall be –
"The LORD is one," and His name one.

~ Zechariah 14:9

This is no dream of an enthusiast, but the declaration of the infallible Word. Jehovah shall be known among all people, and His graciousness shall be acknowledged by every tribe of man.

Today it is far from being so. How much there is of rebellion! Even among professed Christians what diversities of ideas there are about His gospel! One day there shall be one King, one Jehovah, and one name for the living God.

So surely as the Holy Ghost spoke through His prophets, so surely shall the whole earth be filled with the glory of the Lord. Jesus did not die in vain. The Spirit of God works not in vain. The Father's eternal purposes shall not be frustrated. Here, where Satan triumphed, Jesus shall be crowned, and the Lord God Omnipotent shall reign. Let us go our way to our daily work and warfare, made strong in faith.

WITHOUT FEAR OF MAN

*"Then all peoples of the earth shall see that you
are called by the name of the LORD,
and they shall be afraid of you."*

~ *Deuteronomy 28:10*

Then we can have no reason to be afraid of *them*. God can make us so like Himself that men shall be forced to see that we truly belong to the Holy Jehovah.

Be assured that ungodly men have a fear of true saints. They hate them, but they also fear them. Let us pursue the path of truth and uprightness without the slightest tremor. Fear is not for us, but for those who do ill and fight against the Lord of Hosts.

If indeed the name of the Eternal God is named upon us, we are secure; for, as of old, a Roman had but to say *"Romanus sum,"* I am a Roman, and he could claim the protection of all the legions of the vast empire; so everyone who is a man of God has omnipotence as his guardian, and God will sooner empty heaven of angels than leave a saint without defense.

PRESERVED TO WORK'S END

The Lord stood by him and said,
"Be of good cheer, Paul;
for as you have testified for Me in Jerusalem,
so you must also bear witness at Rome."

~ *Acts 23:11*

Are you a witness for the Lord, and are you just now in danger? If the Lord has more witness for you to bear, you will live to bear it. Who is he that can break the vessel that the Lord intends to use?

If there is no more work for you to do for your Master, it cannot distress you that He is about to take you home and put you where you will be beyond the reach of adversaries. Your witness-bearing for Jesus is your chief concern, and you cannot be stopped till it is finished: therefore, be at peace. Cruel slander, wicked misrepresentation, desertion of friends, betrayal by the most trusted one, and whatever else may come cannot hinder the Lord's purpose concerning you.

The Lord stands by you in the night of your sorrow and says, "You must bear witness for Me." Be calm, be filled with joy in the Lord.

THE BIBLE'S SUPREME PLACE

Great peace have those who love Your law,
and nothing causes them to stumble.

~ Psalm 119:165

A true love for the Book will bring us great peace from God and be a great protection to us. Let us live constantly in the society of the law of the Lord, and it will breed in our hearts a restfulness such as nothing else can.

Nothing is a stumbling block to the man who has the Word of God dwelling in him richly. For the fiery trial he is prepared, he is neither stumbled by prosperity, nor crushed by adversity: for he lives beyond the changing circumstances of external life.

When his Lord puts before him some great mystery of the faith which makes others cry, "This is a hard saying!" the believer accepts it without question, for his intellectual difficulties are overcome by his reverent awe of the law of the Lord, which is to him the supreme authority. Lord, work in us this love, this peace, this rest, today.

LOOK AND LIVE

*Then the LORD said to Moses, "Make a fiery serpent,
and set it on a pole; and it shall be that everyone
who is bitten, when he looks at it, shall live."*

~ Numbers 21:8

Jesus, numbered with the transgressors, hangs before us on the cross. A look to Him will heal us of the serpent-bite of sin at once. If you are mourning your sinfulness, note the words, "Everyone who looks at it shall live."

If you look to Jesus you will live. True, you are swelling with the venom and you see no hope. But *there is no hope but this one*. This is no doubtful cure, "Everyone who is bitten, when he looks at it, shall live."

The brazen serpent was not lifted up as a curiosity to be gazed upon by the healthy; but its special purpose was for those who were "bitten." Jesus died as a Savior for sinners. Whether the bite has made you a drunkard, or a thief, or a profane person, a look at the Great Savior will heal you and make you live in holiness and communion with God. Look and live.

CLOSE FELLOWSHIP

*"No more shall every man teach his neighbor,
and every man his brother, saying, 'Know the Lord,'
for they all shall know Me, from the least of
them to the greatest of them," says the Lord.*

~ Jeremiah 31:34

Truly, whatever else we do not know, we know the Lord. This day is this promise true in our experience, and it is not a little one. The least believer among us knows God in Christ Jesus – not as fully as we desire, but yet truly and really we know the Lord.

We not only know doctrines about Him, but we know Him. He is our Father and our Friend. We are acquainted with Him personally. We are on terms of close fellowship with God, and many a happy season do we spend in His holy company.

Flesh and blood has not revealed God to us. Christ Jesus has made known the Father to our hearts. If, then, the Lord has made us know Himself, is not this the fountain of all saving knowledge? To know God is eternal life. O my soul, rejoice in this knowledge and bless God all this day!

HE REMEMBERS NO MORE

*"For I will forgive their iniquity,
and their sin I will remember no more."*

~ *Jeremiah 31:34*

When we know the Lord, we receive the forgiveness of sins. What a joyful discovery is this! How divinely is this promise worded: the Lord promises no more to remember our sins!

Can God forget? He says He will, and He means what He says. He will regard us as though we had never sinned. The great atonement so effectually removed all sin that it is to the mind of God no more in existence.

The Great Lord will not remember our sins so as to punish them, or so as to love us one atom the less because of them. When we are mourning over our transgressions and shortcomings, let us at the same time rejoice that they will never be mentioned against us. God's free pardon makes us anxious never again to grieve Him by disobedience.

THIS BODY TRANSFORMED

*… Who will transform our lowly body that
it may be conformed to His glorious body.*

~ Philippians 3:21

Often when we are racked with pain or we are tempted by the passions of the flesh, we do not think the word "lowly" at all too vigorous a translation. We are lowly, because our bodies ally us with animals, and even link us with the dust!

But our Savior shall change all this. We shall be fashioned like His own body of glory. This will take place in all who believe in Jesus. By faith their souls have been transformed, and their bodies will undergo such a renewal as shall fit them for their regenerated spirits. The thought of this transformation should help us to bear the trials of today and all the woes of the flesh.

In a little while we shall be as Jesus now is – no more aching brows, no more swollen limbs, no more dim eyes, no more fainting hearts. "Conformed to His glorious body." What an expression!

MY CHOICE IS HIS CHOICE

He will choose our inheritance for us.

~ *Psalm 47:4*

Our enemies would allot us a very dreary portion, but we are not left in their hands. The Lord will cause us to stand in our lot, and our place is appointed by His infinite wisdom. A wiser mind than our own arranges our destiny. The ordaining of all things is with God, and we are glad to have it so.

Being conscious of our own folly, we would not desire to rule our own destinies. We feel safer and more at ease when the Lord steers us. Joyfully we leave the painful present and the unknown future with our Father, our Savior, our Comforter.

Today, lay down your wishes at Jesus' feet! If you have of late been somewhat wayward, dismiss your foolish self now, and place the reins in the Lord's hands. It is my freest choice to let Him choose. As a free agent, I elect that He should have absolute sway.

DESIRES OF THE RIGHTEOUS GRANTED

The desire of the righteous will be granted.

~ Proverbs 10:24

Because it is a righteous desire, it is safe for God to grant it. It would not be good for such a promise to be made to the unrighteous.

When righteous men are left to desire unrighteous desires, they will not be granted. But then, these are not their real desires: they are their wanderings or blunders; and they should be refused.

Does the Lord deny us our requests for a time? Let the promise for today encourage us to ask again. Has He denied us altogether? Thank Him still, for it always was our desire that He should deny us if He judged a denial to be best.

Some things we ask very boldly. Our chief desires are for holiness, usefulness, and preparedness for heaven. These are the desires of grace rather than of nature. God will not stint us in these things but will do for us exceeding abundantly. So today, ask largely!

ALL TURNED TO HOLINESS

In that day, "HOLINESS TO THE LORD"
shall be engraved on the bells of the horses.
~ Zechariah 14:20

Happy day when all things shall be consecrated, and the horses' bells shall ring out holiness to the Lord! That day has come to me. Do I not make all things holy to God? Oh, that today my clothes may be vestments, my meals sacraments, my house a temple, my table an altar, my speech incense, and myself a priest! Lord, fulfill Your promise, and let nothing be to me common or unclean.

Let me in faith expect this. As I am the property of Jesus, my Lord may take an inventory of all I have, for it is altogether His own; and I resolve to prove it to be so by the use to which I put it this day.

From morning till evening my bells shall ring: why should they not? All my bells, my music, my mirth shall be turned to holiness and shall ring out the name of "The Happy God."

ENEMIES AT PEACE

When a man's ways please the LORD,
He makes even his enemies to be at peace with him.

~ Proverbs 16:7

I must see that my ways please the Lord, then the Lord will make the wrath of man abate so that it shall not distress me.

He can constrain an enemy from harming me even though he has a mind to do so; as with Laban, who pursued Jacob, but did not dare to touch him. He can subdue an enemy's wrath and make him friendly, as He did with Esau, who met Jacob in a brotherly manner, though Jacob had dreaded that he would smite him. He can convert an adversary into a brother in Christ, as He did with Saul of Tarsus.

Happy is the man whose enemies are made to be to him what the lions were to Daniel in the den, quiet and companionable! When I meet death, the last enemy, I pray that I may be at peace. Only let my great care be to please the Lord in all things.

HE NEVER FAILS

"I will be with you. I will not leave you,
nor forsake you."

~ Joshua 1:5

A life of warfare is before us, but the Lord of Hosts is with us. This promise guarantees us all the wisdom and prudence that we shall need. Have we to contend with cunning and powerful enemies? Here is strength and valor, prowess and victory. Have we a vast heritage to win? By this sign we shall achieve our purpose: the Lord Himself is with us.

On no occasion will the Lord desert us. Happen what may, He will be at our side. Friends drop from us; their help is but an April shower. But God is faithful, Jesus is the same forever, and the Holy Spirit abides in us.

So be calm and hopeful today. Clouds may gather, but the Lord can blow them away. Since God will not fail me, my faith shall not fail, and, as He will not forsake me neither will I forsake Him.

AN EXPERT SEARCHER

For thus says the Lord GOD: "Indeed I Myself
will search for My sheep and seek them out."

~ Ezekiel 34:11

How wonderfully does the Lord find His chosen!
Jesus is a seeking Shepherd as well as a saving
Shepherd. Though many of those His Father gave
Him have gone near to hell's gate, the Lord, by
searching and seeking, discovers them and draws
near to them in grace. He has sought us out: let us
have good hope for those who are laid upon our
hearts in prayer, for He will find them out also.

The Lord repeats this process when any of His
flock stray from the pastures of truth and holiness.
He will, by providence and grace, pursue them into
foreign lands, into abodes of poverty, into dens of
obscurity, into deeps of despair; He will not lose one
that the Father has given Him. It is a point of honor
with Jesus to seek and to save all the flock, without a
single exception.

BY FAITH, NOT FEELING

The just shall live by faith.

~ Romans 1:17

Even if I were perfect, I would not try to live by my righteousness; I would cling to the work of the Lord Jesus, and live by faith in Him and by nothing else.

To live by faith is a far surer and happier thing than to live by feelings or by works. The branch, by living in the vine, lives a better life than it would live by itself, even if it were possible for it to live at all apart from the stem.

To live by clinging to Jesus is a sweet and sacred thing: if even the most just must live in this fashion, how much more must I who am a poor sinner!

Lord, I believe. What else can I do? Trusting You is my life. I will abide by this even to the end.

GOD REPAYS

He who has pity on the poor lends to the LORD,
and He will pay back what he has given.

~ Proverbs 19:17

We are to give to the poor, not to be seen and applauded, but out of pure sympathy and compassion.

We must not expect to get anything back, not even gratitude; but we should regard what we have done as a loan to the Lord. He undertakes the obligation; and, if we look to Him in the matter, we must not look to the second party.

What an honor the Lord bestows upon us when He condescends to borrow of us! Let us not make it a paltry pittance but a heavy amount. The next needy man that comes this way, let us help him.

As for repayment we can hardly think of it, and yet here is the Lord's note of hand. Blessed be His name, His promise to pay is better than gold and silver. Has any reader neglected the poor? Poor soul. May the Lord forgive him.

POWER TO RAISE

The LORD opens the eyes of the blind;
the LORD raises those who are bowed down.

~ Psalm 146:8

Am I bowed down? Then let me urge this word of grace before the Lord. It is His promise, His delight, to raise up those who are bowed down.

Is it sin, and a consequent depression of spirit, which now distresses me? Then the work of Jesus is, in this case, made and provided to raise me up into rest.

Is it a sad bereavement, or a great fall in circumstances? Here again the Comforter has undertaken to console; He has made it His peculiar care.

Some are so bowed down that only Jesus can loose them from their infirmity; but He can, and He will, do it. He can raise us up to health, to hope, to happiness.

We who are bowed down and sorrowful shall be set on high. What an honor to be raised up by the Lord! It is worthwhile to be bowed down that we may experience His upraising power.

NO FEAR OF DEATH

"He who has an ear, let him hear what the Spirit says to the churches. He who overcomes shall not be hurt by the second death."

~ Revelation 2:11

The first death we must endure, but let us not fear it, since Jesus has transformed death into a passage leading to glory.

The thing to be feared is not the first, but the second death; not the parting of the soul from the body, but the final separation of the entire man from God. This is death indeed – it kills all peace, joy, happiness, and hope. Such a death is far worse than ceasing to be: it is existence without the life that makes existence worth having.

If by God's grace we fight on to the end and conquer in the glorious war, no second death can lay its chilly finger upon us. Eternal life is worth a life's battle. To escape the hurt of the second death is a thing worth struggling for throughout a lifetime.

Lord, give us faith so that we may overcome, though sin and Satan dog our heels!

CONDITION OF BLESSING

*"Bring all the tithes into the storehouse, that there may
be food in My house, and try Me now in this,"
says the LORD of hosts, "If I will not open for
you the windows of heaven and pour out
for you such blessing that there will not
be room enough to receive it."*

~ *Malachi 3:10*

Many read and plead this promise without noticing
the condition upon which the blessing is promised.
We cannot expect heaven to be opened or blessing
poured out unless we pay our dues to the Lord our
God and to His cause. There would be no lack of
funds for holy purposes if all professing Christians
paid their fair share.

If there is no temporal meat for God's servants,
we need not wonder if their ministry has but little
food in it for our souls. When missions pine for
means, and the work of the Lord is hindered by an
empty treasury, how can we look for a large amount
of soul prosperity? What have I given of late? Let me
give my Lord Jesus His tithe by helping the poor and
aiding His work.

WHAT TO LEAVE CHILDREN

The righteous man walks in his integrity;
his children are blessed after him.

~ Proverbs 20:7

If we walk before the Lord in integrity, we shall do more to bless our descendants than if we bequeathed them large estates. A father's holy life is a rich legacy for his sons.

The upright man leaves his heirs his example, and this in itself is a mine of true wealth. How many men may trace their success in life to the example of their parents!

Above all, a righteous father leaves his children his prayers and the blessing of a prayer-hearing God, and these make our offspring to be favored among the sons of men. God will save them even after we are dead.

Our integrity may be God's means of saving our sons and daughters. If they see the truth of our religion proved by our lives, it may be that they will believe in Jesus for themselves. Lord, fulfill this word to my household!

GRACIOUS DEALING

The LORD your God will
bless you in all that you do.

~ Deuteronomy 15:18

A master was to give his bondservant liberty in due time, and was to start him in life with a liberal portion, heartily and cheerfully, so the Lord promised to bless the generous act.

The spirit of this precept binds us to treat work people well. We ought to remember how the Lord has dealt with us and therefore we should deal graciously with others. It becomes those to be generous who are the children of a gracious God. How can we expect our great Master to bless us in our business if we oppress those who serve us?

To be blessed in all that we do is to be blessed indeed. The Lord will send us this partly in prosperity, partly in content of mind, and partly in a sense of His favor, which is the best of all blessings. God's blessing is more than a fortune. It makes rich and adds no sorrow.

GOD FINISHES HIS WORK

*The LORD will perfect
that which concerns me.*

~ Psalm 138:8

He who has begun will carry on the work that is being wrought within me. What is now good, but not perfect, the Lord will watch over, preserve, and carry out to completion. This is a great comfort, for I fail daily, and have only held on because the Lord has helped me.

The Lord will continue to bless me. He will perfect my faith, my love, my character, my life's work. He will do this because He has begun a work in me. He never leaves a work unfinished; this would not be for His glory, nor would it be like Him. He knows how to accomplish His gracious design.

Though my own evil nature, the world, and the devil all conspire to hinder Him, I do not doubt His promise. He will fulfill His purpose for me. Lord, let Your gracious work make some advance this day!

IT BECOMES NATURAL

*"I will dwell in them and walk among them.
I will be their God, and they shall be My people."*

~ 2 Corinthians 6:16

Here is a *mutual interest*. Each belongs to each. God is the portion of His people, and the chosen people are the portion of their God. God is our chief possession, and we are His peculiar treasure.

This happy condition of mutual interest leads to *mutual consideration*. God will always think of His own people, and they will always think of Him.

This day my God will perform all things for me; what can I do for Him? My thoughts ought to run toward Him, for He thinks on me. Let me make sure that it is so. This, again, leads to *mutual fellowship*. God dwells in us, and we dwell in Him; He walks with us and we walk with God.

May I treat the Lord as my God: trust Him and serve Him, as His Godhead deserves! To love, worship, adore, and obey Jehovah in spirit and in truth! This is my heart's desire. When I shall attain to it, I shall have found my heaven.

FORGET AND FORGIVE

Do not say, "I will recompense evil";
wait for the LORD, and He will save you.

~ *Proverbs 20:22*

Be not in haste. Let your anger cool. Say nothing and do nothing to avenge yourself, as that will not show the spirit of the Lord. It is nobler to forgive, and let the offense pass. To let an injury rankle and to meditate revenge is to keep old wounds open.

Perhaps you feel like you must do something or be considered a loser; then do what this morning's promise advises, "Wait for the LORD." Wait on the Lord; tell Him your grievance, this itself will ease your burdened mind. Besides, there is the promise, "He will save you."

God will find a way of deliverance for you. How He will do it, we cannot guess, but do it He will. Don't get into petty quarrels and cover yourself with filth by wrestling with the unclean. Be no more angry. Leave your case with the Judge of all.

THE OVERCOMER'S REWARD

*"He who has an ear, let him hear what the Spirit says
to the churches. To him who overcomes I will give
some of the hidden manna to eat. And I will
give him a white stone, and on the stone
a new name written which no one knows
except him who receives it."*

~ *Revelation 2:17*

My heart, be stirred up to persevere in the holy war, for the reward of victory is great. There is reserved for us in Christ a higher degree of spiritual life, and food for it, which is hidden. In the golden pot that was laid up in the ark, there was a portion of manna hidden away, which though kept for ages, never grew stale.

The highest life of the believer is hid with Christ, in God. We shall come to it soon. Being made victorious through the grace of our Lord, we shall eat of the King's meat. We shall feed upon Jesus. He is our "hidden manna." He is all in all to us in our highest, as well as in our lowest, estate. He helps us to fight, gives us the victory, and then is Himself our reward. Lord, help me to overcome.

May

FULL OF SONG

*The mountains and the hills shall break forth
into singing before you, and all the trees
of the field shall clap their hands.*

~ Isaiah 55:12

When sin is pardoned, our greatest sorrow ends, and our truest pleasure begins. Such is the joy that the Lord bestows upon His reconciled ones that it overflows and fills all nature with delight.

The material world has latent music in it, and a renewed heart knows how to bring it out and make it vocal. Mountains and hills are the bass of the chorus, while the trees of the wood and all things that have life take up the air of the melodious song.

When God's Word is made to prosper among us, and souls are saved, then everything seems full of song. Then it seems as if rocks and hills, and woods and fields echoed our joy-notes and turned the world into an orchestra. Lord, on this happy May day, lead me out into Your tuneful world as rich in praise as a lark in full song.

SPIRITUAL SOWING

He who sows to the Spirit will
of the Spirit reap everlasting life.

~ Galatians 6:8

Sowing looks like a losing business; we put corn into the ground never to see it again. Yet if we sow to the Spirit by studying to live unto God, seeking to obey His will, and promoting His honor, we shall not sow in vain. Life shall be our reward, even everlasting life. This we enjoy here as we enter into the knowledge of God, communion with God, and enjoyment of God. This life flows on like an ever-deepening river till it bears us to the ocean of infinite felicity, where the life of God is ours forever.

Let us not sow to our flesh, for the harvest will be corruption, but let us live for the highest, purest, and most spiritual ends, seeking to honor the Lord by obeying His most gracious Spirit. What a harvest will that be when we reap life everlasting! What sheaves of endless bliss will be reaped!

LISTEN FOR THE SIGNAL

It shall be, when you hear the sound of marching in the tops of the mulberry trees, then you shall advance quickly. For then the LORD will go out before you to strike the camp of the Philistines.

~ 2 Samuel 5:24

There are signs of the Lord's moving which should move us. Then is the time for us to be more than ever astir. It is ours to fight the Philistines at all times; but when the Lord Himself goes out before us, we should be especially valiant in the war.

The breeze stirred the tops of the trees, and David and his men took this to signal an onslaught; and at their advance, the Lord Himself smote the Philistines. Today may the Lord give us an opening to speak for Him with our friends! Let us be on the watch to avail ourselves of the hopeful opening when it comes.

This may be a day of good tidings; a season of soul winning. Let us keep our ear open to hear the rustle of the wind, and our minds ready to obey the signal. Since the Lord goes before us, we dare not hold back.

VICTORY IN DISTRESS

*Do not rejoice over me, my enemy; when I fall,
I will arise; when I sit in darkness,
the LORD will be a light to me.*

~ Micah 7:8

This may express the feeling of a man or woman downtrodden and oppressed. Our enemy may put out our light for a season, but if we are trusting in the Lord and holding fast our integrity, our season of downcasting and darkness will soon be over. The insults of the foe are only for a moment. The Lord will soon turn their laughter into lamentation, and our sighing into singing.

What if the great enemy of souls should for a while triumph over us, as he has triumphed over better men than us, yet let us take heart, for we shall overcome him before long.

We shall rise from our fall, for our God has not fallen, and He will lift us up. We shall not abide in darkness, although for the moment we sit in it, for our Lord is the fountain of light, and He will soon bring us a joyful day.

WHY REMAIN CAPTIVE?

*The LORD your God will bring you
back from captivity.*

~ *Deuteronomy 30:3*

What a bondage it is when a child of God is held in chains by Satan, robbed of his power in prayer and his delight in the Lord!

If this has already happened, do not despair – we cannot be held in slavery forever. The Lord has paid too high a price for our redemption to leave us in the enemy's hand. The way to freedom is to return to the Lord. Where we first found salvation, we shall find it again.

At the foot of Christ's cross confessing sin, we shall find pardon and deliverance. Moreover, the Lord will have us obey all that He has commanded us, and we must do this with all our heart and all our soul, and then our captivity shall end.

Often depression and misery are removed as soon as we quit our idols and bow ourselves in obedience before the living God. Lord, save us from captivity!

CURE FOR ENVY

*Do not let your heart envy sinners, but be zealous for
the fear of the LORD all the day; for surely there is
a hereafter, and your hope will not be cut off.*

~ Proverbs 23:17-18

When we see the wicked prosper we are apt to envy
them and think that they have the best of it. This
is foolish and sinful. If we knew them better, and
especially if we remembered their end, we would
pity them.

The cure for envy lies in living under a constant
sense of the divine presence, worshiping God, and
communing with Him all the day long. True religion
lifts the soul into a higher region. The more of
heaven there is in our lives, the less of earth we shall
covet. The fear of God casts out envy.

The deathblow of envy is a calm consideration
of the future. What is the prosperous sinner the better for his prosperity when judgment overtakes him?
As for the godly man, his end is peace and blessedness, and none can rob him of his joy; therefore, let
him forego envy and be filled with sweet content.

LET NO EVIL REMAIN

None of the accursed things shall remain in your hand,
that the LORD may turn from the fierceness of His anger
and show you mercy, have compassion on you
and multiply you, just as He swore to your fathers.

~ Deuteronomy 13:17

Israel must conquer idolatrous cities and destroy all the spoil, regarding all that had been polluted by idolatry as an accursed thing to be burned with fire. Now, sin of all sorts must be treated by Christians in the same manner. We must not allow a single evil habit to remain. We regard this as a fruit of the grace of God, which we would on no account miss.

When we multiply our efforts against iniquity, the Lord multiplies our blessings. The way of peace, of growth, of safety, of joy in Christ Jesus will be found by following out these words, "None of the accursed things shall remain in your hand."

Lord, purify me this day. Compassion, prosperity, increase, and joy will surely be given to those who put away sin with solemn resolution.

HELP WANTED

"You also go into the vineyard,
and whatever is right you will receive."

~ Matthew 20:7

Yes, here is work in Christ's vineyard for old bodies. It is the eleventh hour, and yet He will let us work. What great grace is this! Surely every old man ought to jump at this invitation!

After men are advanced in years, nobody wants to employ them; they go from shop to shop, and employers look at their gray hairs and shake their heads. But Jesus will engage old people and give them good wages too! Lord, help the aged to enlist in Your service without an hour's delay.

But will the Lord pay wages to worn-out old men? Do not doubt it. He will grant present comfort and future rest: strength equal to your day, and a vision of glory when the night of death comes on. All these the Lord Jesus will as freely give to the aged convert as to one who enters His service in his youth.

TRUST MEANS JOY

*Our heart shall rejoice in Him,
because we have trusted in His holy name.*

~ Psalm 33:21

The root of faith produces the flower of heart joy. We may not at first rejoice, but we will. We trust the Lord when we are sad, and in due season, He so answers our confidence that our faith turns to fruition and we rejoice in the Lord.

The psalmist's assurance in this verse is a promise, held out in the hands of holy confidence. If we do not rejoice at this moment, yet we shall do so, as surely as David's God is our God.

Let us meditate upon the Lord's holy name, that we may trust Him the better and rejoice the more readily. He is in character holy, just, true, gracious, faithful, and unchanging.

Jehovah Jireh will provide; Jehovah Shalom will send peace; Jehovah Tsidkenu will justify; Jehovah Shammah will be forever near; and Jehovah Nissi will conquer every foe. They who know Your name will trust You and will rejoice in You, Lord.

FEAR ONLY GOD

We may boldly say: "The LORD is my helper;
I will not fear. What can man do to me?"

~ Hebrews 13:6

Because God will never leave nor forsake us, we will never be left without a friend, a treasure, and a dwelling place. This assurance may make us feel quite independent of men.

Under such high patronage, we do not feel tempted to cringe before our fellow men and ask of them permission to call our lives our own; but what we say, we boldly say and defy contradiction.

He who fears God has nothing else to fear. We should stand in such awe of the living Lord that all the threats that can be used by the proudest persecutor should have no more effect upon us than the whistling of the wind. So we must bear the world's scorn. It breaks no bones. God helping us, let us be bold; and when the world rages let it rage, but let us not fear it.

WAIT FOR THE FINALS

Gad, a troop shall tramp upon him,
but he shall triumph at last.

~ Genesis 49:19

Some of us have been like the tribe of Gad. Our adversaries were too many for us; they came upon us like a troop, and for a moment they overcame us, and they exulted greatly because of their temporary victory.

Being overcome is very painful, and we should have despaired if we had not by faith believed the second line of our Father's benediction, "He shall triumph at last." "All's well that ends well," said the world's poet; and he spoke the truth. A war is to be judged, not by first successes, but by that which happens at the end. The Lord will give to truth and righteousness, victory "at last"; and, as Mr. Bunyan says, that means forever; for nothing can come after the last.

What we need is patient perseverance to go through with suffering till we can say, "It is finished." Hallelujah! We believe the promise. "He shall triumph at last."

SERVANTS HONORED

Whoever keeps the fig tree will eat its fruit;
so he who waits on his master will be honored.

~ Proverbs 27:18

He who tends the fig tree has figs for his pains, and he who waits on a good master has honor as his reward. To serve the Lord is to keep a fig tree of the sweetest figs. His service is in itself delight, continuance in it is promotion, success in it is blessedness below, and the reward for it is glory above.

Angels, who are now our servitors, will bear us home when our day's work is done. Heaven, where Jesus is, will be our honorable mansion; eternal bliss, our honorable portion, and the Lord Himself, our honorable companion. Who can imagine the full meaning of this promise, "He who waits on his master will be honored"?

Lord, help me to wait upon You. Let me leave all idea of honor to the hour when You Yourself will honor me. May Your Holy Spirit make me a lowly patient worker and waiter!

DAY IS AT HAND

"I will give him the morning star."

~ *Revelation 2:28*

Until the daybreak and the shadows flee away, what a blessing it is to see in Jesus "the morning star!"

It is best to see Jesus as the sun; but when we cannot do so, the next best thing is to see Him as the star that prophesies the day and shows that eternal light is near.

If I am not today all that I hope to be, yet I see Jesus, that assures me that I shall one day be like Him. If I have not at this hour all the joy I could desire, yet I shall have it; for as surely as I see the morning star I shall see the day. The morning star is never far from the sun.

Do you hold fast that truth, grace, hope, and love that the Lord has given you? Then in this, you have the dawn of coming glory.

SURGERY FOR HEALING

"Come, and let us return to the LORD; for He has torn,
but He will heal us; He has stricken,
but He will bind us up."

~ Hosea 6:1

It is the Lord's way to tear before He heals. This is the honest love of His heart, and the sure surgery of His hand. He also bruises before He binds up, or else it would be uncertain work. The law comes before the gospel; the sense of need before the supply of it. Is the reader now under the convincing, crushing hand of the Spirit? This is a preliminary to healing and binding up.

Do not despair, but come to the Lord with all your wounds, bruises, and sores. He alone can heal, and He delights to do it. Let us show Him our gaping wounds, and beseech Him to know His own work and complete it. Will a surgeon make an incision, and then leave his patient to bleed to death? Will the Lord pull down our old house, and then refuse to build us a better one? Never!

GOD'S HIGH PLACES

"I will set him on high,
because he has known My name."

~ Psalm 91:14

Does the Lord say this to me? Yes, if I have known His name. Blessed be the Lord, I am no stranger to Him. I have tried Him, and proved Him, and known Him; and therefore, do I trust Him.

I know His name as a sin-hating God, for He will never wink at evil. But I also know Him as the sin-pardoning God, for He has forgiven me all trespasses. His name is faithfulness, and I know it, for He has never forsaken me.

This knowledge is a gift of grace, and the Lord makes it to be the reason why He grants another grace gift – namely, setting on high. This is grace upon grace.

Observe that if we climb on high, the position may be dangerous; but if the Lord sets us there, it is safe. When God sets us on high, Satan himself cannot pull us down.

WE RECEIVE AS WE GIVE

"Blessed are the merciful,
for they shall obtain mercy."

~ *Matthew 5:7*

It is not right that the man who will not forgive should be forgiven, nor shall he who will not give to the poor have his own wants relieved. God will measure to us with our own bushels. "Judgment is without mercy to the one who has shown no mercy" (James 2:13).

This day let us try to give and to forgive. Let us mind the two bears – bear and forbear. Let us be kind, gentle, and tender. Let us not drive hard bargains, or pick foolish quarrels, or be too difficult to please.

Surely we wish to be blessed: let us be merciful, that we may have mercy. Let us fulfill the condition, that we may earn the beatitude. Is it not a pleasant duty to be kind? Is there not much more sweetness in it than in being angry and ungenerous? Why, there is blessedness in the thing itself!

NO NEED TO STINT

"The upright shall have good things in possession."

~ *Proverbs 28:10* KJV

This is a remarkable promise. We are accustomed to think of our good things as in reversion, but here it says we shall have them in possession.

All the malice and cunning of our enemies cannot work our destruction. Our inheritance is so entailed upon us that we shall not be kept out of it.

But what have we now? We have the love of God set upon us. We have power with God in prayer in all time of need. We have the providence of God to watch over us, the angels of God to minister to us, and, above all, the Spirit of God to dwell in us. In fact, all things are ours. "Things present or things to come – all are yours" (1 Cor. 3:22). Jesus is ours. Hallelujah. Let us not pine and whine, since we have good things in possession. Let us rejoice in our God all the day.

LOSSES OVERCOME

*"I will restore to you the years that
the swarming locust has eaten."*

~ Joel 2:25

Yes, those wasted years over which we sigh shall be restored to us. God can give us such plentiful days that we shall crowd into the remainder of our days as much of service as will be some recompense for those years of unregeneracy over which we mourn in humble penitence.

The locusts of backsliding, worldliness, and luke-warmness are now viewed by us as a terrible plague. We can raise such harvests of spiritual graces as shall make our former barrenness disappear. Through rich grace we can turn to account our bitter experiences and use it to warn others.

If we are the more watchful, zealous, and tender, we shall gain by our lamentable losses. The wasted years, by a miracle of love, can be restored. Let us believe for and live for it; and we may yet realize it. Lord, aid us by Your grace.

WE MAY SPEAK FOR GOD

Therefore thus says the LORD: "If you return, then
I will bring you back; you shall stand before Me;
if you take out the precious from the vile,
you shall be as My mouth."

~ Jeremiah 15:19

Poor Jeremiah! The weeping prophet was one of the choicest servants of God and honored by Him above many, yet he was hated for speaking the truth. The word which was so sweet to him was bitter to his hearers, yet he was accepted of his Lord. He was commanded to abide in his faithfulness, and then the Lord would continue to speak through him, "You shall be as My mouth."

What an honor! Should not every believer covet it? We shall speak sure, pure truth; and we shall speak it with power. Our word shall not return void; it shall be a blessing to those who receive it. Our lips shall feed many. We shall arouse the sleeping and call the dead to life.

Dear reader, pray that it may be so with all the sent servants of our Lord.

WE DARE NOT DOUBT

"I will go before you and make the crooked
places straight; I will break in pieces the
gates of bronze and cut the bars of iron."

~ *Isaiah 45:2*

This was for Cyrus; but it is also for the Lord's followers. Let us go forward by faith, and our way will be cleared for us. Crooks and turns of human craft and satanic subtlety shall be straightened for us. The gates and iron bars will be destroyed. We shall not need the battering ram: the Lord Himself will do the impossible for us.

Let us not fear. Let us press onward in the path of duty, for the Lord has said, "I will go before You." Ours is not to reason why; ours is but to dare and dash forward. It is the Lord God's work, and He will enable us to do it: all impediments must yield before Him.

Those who serve God have infinite resources. The way is clear to faith, though barred to human strength. When Jehovah says, "I will," as He does twice in this promise, we dare not doubt.

RAIN WITHOUT CLOUDS? NEVER!

If the clouds are full of rain,
they empty themselves upon the earth.

~ Ecclesiastes 11:3

Why do we dread the clouds that now darken our sky? True, for a while they hide the sun, but the sun is not quenched; he will shine out again before long. Meanwhile those black clouds are filled with rain, and the blacker they are, the more likely they are to yield plentiful showers. How can we have rain without clouds?

Our troubles have always brought us blessings, and they always will. Our God may drench us with grief, but He will not drown us with wrath; He will refresh us with mercy. Let us not worry about the clouds, but sing because May flowers are brought to us through the April clouds and showers.

O Lord, the clouds are the dust of Your feet! How near You are in the cloudy and dark day! Faith sees the clouds emptying themselves and making the little hills rejoice on every side.

SONG OF CONFIDENCE

Though I walk in the midst of trouble, You will
revive me; You will stretch out Your hand
against the wrath of my enemies,
and Your right hand will save me.

~ Psalm 138:7

Wretched walking in the midst of trouble. No, blessed walking, since there is a special promise for it. What does my Lord teach me here to say? "You will revive me." I shall have more life, more energy, more faith. Is it not often so that trouble revives us like a breath of cold air?

How angry are my enemies and especially the archenemy! Shall I stretch forth my hand and fight my foes? There is no need, for my God will use His far-reaching arm, and He will deal with them far better than I could? He will with His own right hand of power and wisdom save me, and what more can I desire?

Come, my heart, talk this promise over until it becomes a song of confidence, the solace of your holiness. Pray to be revived and leave the rest with the Lord, who performs all things for you.

FULL RELIANCE ON GOD

He will deliver the needy when he cries,
the poor also, and him who has no helper.

~ *Psalm 72:12*

Let the needy reader take to crying at once, for this will be his wisdom. Do not cry in the ears of friends, the nearest way is to go straight to God, and let your cry come up before Him. Straight forward makes the best runner: run to the Lord, and not to secondary causes.

Even for temporal mercies you may wait upon God, for He cares for His children in these temporary concerns. As for spiritual necessities, which are the heaviest of all, the Lord will hear your cry and will deliver you and supply you.

O poor friend, try your rich God. O helpless one, lean on His help. He has never failed me, and I am sure He will never fail you. Come with no plea but His grace. Jesus is King; will He let you perish of want? Never! Did you forget this?

ONE A MAJORITY!

One man of you shall chase a thousand,
for the LORD your God is He who fights
for you, as He promised you.

~ Joshua 23:10

Why count heads? One man with God is a majority though there be a thousand on the other side. The Lord's hosts are never too few.

When God would found a nation, He called Abram alone and blessed him. When He would vanquish proud Pharaoh, He used only Moses and Aaron. The "one man ministry" has been far more used of the Lord than trained bands with their officers. Did all the Israelites together slay so many as Samson alone? Saul and his hosts slew their thousands, but David his ten thousands.

If we have God with us; what are multitudes of men? One shepherd's dog can drive before him a great flock of sheep. If the Lord sent you, His strength will accomplish His divine purpose. Therefore, rely on the promise, and be courageous.

GOD'S TREASURY

The LORD will open to you
His good treasure.

~ *Deuteronomy 28:12*

This refers first to the rain. The Lord will give this in its season. Rain is the emblem of all those celestial refreshings that the Lord is ready to bestow upon His people. Oh, for a copious shower to refresh the Lord's heritage!

We seem to think that God's treasury can only be opened by a great prophet like Elijah, but it is not so, for this promise is to all the faithful. You, too, may see heaven opened. Ask what you desire and you will not be denied, if you abide in Christ and His words abide in you.

As yet you have not known all the Lord's treasures, but He shall open them up to your understanding. Only the Lord Himself can do this for you, but here is His promise. And if you will hear His voice and obey His will, His riches in glory by Christ Jesus shall be yours.

COMMON THINGS BLESSED

*You shall serve the L*ORD *your God,*
and He will bless your bread and your water.

~ Exodus 23:25

What a privilege to have the blessing of the Lord resting upon us in all things! Our most common things become blessed when we ourselves are consecrated to the Lord. Our Lord Jesus took bread and blessed it; behold, we also eat of blessed bread. Jesus blessed water and made it wine. The divine blessing is on the man of God in everything, and it shall abide with him at every time.

With God at our table, we not only ask a blessing, but we have one. It is not only at the altar but also at the table that He blesses us. He serves those well who serve Him well.

This table blessing is not of debt, but of grace. Indeed, there is a trebled grace: He grants us grace to serve Him; by His grace He feeds us with bread; and then in His grace blesses it.

AS THE LIFE, SO THE FRUIT

If these things are yours and abound,
you will be neither barren nor unfruitful
in the knowledge of our Lord Jesus Christ.

~ 2 Peter 1:8

If we desire to glorify our Lord by fruitfulness, we must have certain things within us; for nothing can come out of us which is not first within us.

We must begin with faith, which is the groundwork of all the virtues; and then diligently add to it virtue, knowledge, temperance, patience, godliness and brotherly love. All these put together will cause us to produce – as our life fruit – the clusters of usefulness, and we shall not be mere idle knowers, but real doers of the Word. These holy things must abound or we shall be barren. Fruit is the overflow of life, and we must be full before we can flow over.

For real usefulness, graces are better than gifts. As the man is, so is his work. If we would *do* better we must *be* better. Let the text be a gentle hint to unfruitful professors, and to myself also.

REMIND GOD OF HIS PROMISE

You said, "I will surely treat you well."

~ *Genesis 32:12*

This is a sure way of prevailing with the Lord; humbly remind Him of what He has said. Our faithful God will never take back His word or leave it unfulfilled; yet He loves to be enquired of by His people and put in mind of His promise. This is refreshing to their memories, reviving to their faith, and renewing to their hope.

God's Word is given not for His sake, but for ours. His purposes are settled, and He needs nothing to bind Him to His design of doing His people good. But He wishes us to plead it and say to Him, "You said."

"I will surely treat you well" is the essence of all the Lord's gracious sayings. He will do us good; real good, lasting good, only good, every good. With this promise in our hearts, we need not fear. If the Lord will do us good, who can do us hurt?

FISHERS, FOLLOW ME

*Jesus said to them, "Follow Me, and
I will make you become fishers of men."*

~ Mark 1:17

Oh, how we long to be successful fishers for Jesus! But we are tempted to try methods that Jesus would never have tried. Shall we yield to this suggestion of the enemy? If so, we may splash the water, but we shall never take the fish. We must follow after Jesus if we would succeed. Sensational methods, entertainments, and so forth – are these coming after Jesus?

We must keep to our preaching as our Master did, for by this means, souls are saved. We must preach our Lord's doctrine and proclaim a full and free gospel, for this is the net in which souls are taken. We must preach with His gentleness, boldness, and love; for this is the secret of success with human hearts. We must work under divine anointing, depending upon the sacred Spirit. Thus, coming after Jesus, and not running before Him, or aside from Him, we shall be fishers of men.

HOLY FORESIGHT

Jesus said to him, "It is as you said. Nevertheless,
I say to you, hereafter you will see the Son of Man
sitting at the right hand of the Power,
and coming on the clouds of heaven."

~ Matthew 26:64

Lord, You were in Your lowest state when, before Your persecutors, You were made to stand beyond Your present humiliation into Your future glory. What words are these, "Nevertheless … hereafter!"

Instead of weakness, You have all power; instead of shame, all glory; instead of derision, all worship. Your cross has not dimmed the splendor of Your crown. Rather, You are the more exalted and honored because of Your sufferings.

So, Lord, I also would take courage from the "hereafter." I would forget the present tribulation in the future triumph. Help me to think more and more of the hereafter and less of today. I shall be with You soon and behold Your glory. Therefore, I am not ashamed, but say in my inmost soul, "Nevertheless … hereafter."

BE OF GOOD CHEER

"In the world you will have tribulation;
but be of good cheer, I have overcome the world."

~ John 16:33

My Lord's words are true; I have my share of tribulation beyond all doubt. How can I look to be at home in the enemy's country, joyful while in exile, or comfortable in a wilderness? This is not my rest. This is the place of the furnace, the forge, and the hammer.

He bids me "be of good cheer." Yet I am too easily downcast. My spirit sinks when I am sorely tried. But I must not give way to this feeling. When my Lord God bids me cheer up, I must not declare to be cast down.

What is the argument that He uses to encourage me? His own victory! He says, "I have overcome the world." His battle was much more severe than mine. Why do I despair of overcoming? The enemy has been overcome. I fight with a beaten foe. Therefore, I am of good cheer and sing unto my conquering Lord.

June

GOD'S PROMISE KEEPS

*Cast your bread upon the waters,
for you will find it after many days.*

~ *Ecclesiastes 11:1*

Do not expect to see an immediate reward for the good you do. The Egyptian casts his seed upon the Nile, where it might seem a waste. But in due time the flood subsides, the seed sinks into the fertile mud, and a harvest is produced. Let us today do good to the unthankful and the evil, the careless and the obstinate. Unlikely waters may cover hopeful soil, but nowhere shall our labor be in vain in the Lord.

We cast the bread upon the waters; but it remains with God to fulfill the promise, "You will find it." He will not let His promise fail. His good word shall live and shall be found by us. Perhaps not just yet, but some day, we shall reap what we have sown. "After many days," says the Scripture, and in many instances those days run into months and years, yet God's promise will keep.

IMMEDIATE FREEDOM

"Now I will break off his yoke from you,
and burst your bonds apart."

~ *Nahum 1:13*

The Assyrian was allowed for a season to oppress the Lord's people, but there came a time for his power to be broken. Just so, many a heart is held in bondage by Satan. To such prisoners of hope may the word of the Lord come at once, "Now I will break off his yoke from you."

See! The Lord promises a present deliverance: "Now I will break off his yoke from you." Believe for immediate freedom; and, according to your faith, so shall it be. When God says "now," let no man say tomorrow.

See how complete the rescue is to be; it is a display of divine force that guarantees that the oppressor shall not return. His yoke is broken; we cannot again be bowed down by its weight. His bonds are burst apart; they can no longer hold us. Come, Lord, and set free Your captives, according to Your word.

SUREFOOTEDNESS

The LORD God is my strength; He will make
my feet like deer's feet, and He will
make me walk on my high hills.

~ *Habakkuk 3:19*

The prophet Habakkuk had to traverse the deep places of poverty and famine, but he went downhill without slipping, for the Lord gave him *standing*. By and by, he was called to the high places of the hills of conflict; and he was no more afraid to go up than to go down.

The Lord not only lent him *strength*, He was his strength. Think of that: the Almighty God Himself becomes our strength!

Note that the Lord also gave him *surefootedness*. The deer leaps over rock and crag, never missing its foothold. Our Lord will give us grace to follow the most difficult paths of duty without stumbling.

One of these days we shall be called to higher places still. Up yonder we shall climb, even to the mount of God, the high places where the shining ones are gathered. With feet of faith we shall ascend the hill of the Lord!

EXCEEDINGLY PRECIOUS

"They shall be Mine," says the LORD of hosts,
"on the day that I make them My jewels."

~ Malachi 3:17

Are you among the precious things of Jesus? You are precious to Him if He is precious to you, and you shall be His "on that day," if He is yours on this day.

In the days of Malachi, the chosen of the Lord were accustomed to so converse with each other that God Himself listened to their talk. He even took notes of it and made a book of it, which he lodged in His record office. Pleased with their conversation, He was also pleased with them. Pause and ask yourself: If Jesus were to listen to my talk, would He be pleased with it? Is it to His glory?

What an honor for us to be reckoned by the Lord to be His crown jewels! Jesus bought us, sought us, and has so far wrought us to His image that we shall be fought for by Him with all His might.

IS THERE A DIFFERENCE?

*Against none of the children of Israel shall
a dog move its tongue, against man or beast,
that you may know that the LORD does make
a difference between the Egyptians and Israel.*

~ *Exodus 11:7*

God even has power over the tongues of dogs! He can prevent an Egyptian dog from worrying the lambs of Israel's flock. Does God silence dogs, and doggish ones among men, and the great dog at hell's gate? Then let us go forward without fear.

If He lets dogs move their tongues, He can also stop their teeth. They may make a dreadful noise but will do us no real harm. How delightful to move among enemies and perceive that God makes them to be at peace with us! Like Daniel in the den of lions, we are unhurt amid destroyers.

May this word of the Lord be true to me today! Does the dog worry me? I will tell my Lord about him. Give me peace, God, and let me see Your hand so distinctly in it that I may clearly perceive the difference that Your grace has made between me and the ungodly!

HE ALWAYS LISTENS

The LORD has heard my supplication;
the LORD will receive my prayer.

~ *Psalm 6:9*

The experience here recorded is mine. I know that God is true. In very wonderful ways He has answered the prayers of His servant many a time. And He is hearing my present supplication and not turning away His ear from me. Blessed be His holy name!

So the promise, which lies sleeping in the psalmist's believing confidence, is also mine. Let me grasp it by the hand of faith: "The LORD will receive my prayer." He will accept it, think of it, and grant it in the way and time which His loving wisdom judges to be best.

I bring my poor prayer in my hand to the great King, and He gives me audience and graciously receives my petition. My enemies will not listen to me, but my Lord will. They ridicule my tearful prayers, but my Lord does not; He receives my prayer into His ear and His heart.

THE SAFEST PLACE

"I give them eternal life, and they shall never perish;
neither shall anyone snatch them out of My hand."

~ John 10:28

We believe in the eternal security of the saint. First, because they are Christ's, and He will never lose the sheep that He has bought with His blood, and received of His Father.

Next, because He gives them eternal life, and if it be eternal, well then, it is eternal, and there can be no end to hell, heaven, or God. If spiritual life can die out, it is manifestly not eternal life, but temporary life. But the Lord speaks of eternal life, and that effectually shuts out the possibility of an end.

Observe further that the Lord expressly says, "They shall never perish." As long as words have a meaning, this secures believers from perishing.

Then, to make the matter complete, He declares that His people are in His hand, and He defies all their enemies to pluck them out of it. We are safe in the Savior's grasp.

So dismiss carnal fear and rest peacefully in the hollow of the Redeemer's hand.

WISDOM FOR THE ASKING

*If any of you lacks wisdom, let him ask of God,
who gives to all liberally and without reproach,
and it will be given to him.*

~ James 1:5

If any of you lack wisdom. There is no "if" in the matter, for I am sure I lack it. What do I know? How can I guide my own way? How can I direct others? Lord, I am a mass of folly, and wisdom I have none.

You say, "Let him ask of God." Lord, I now ask. Here at Your footstool, I ask to be furnished with heavenly wisdom for this day's perplexities and simplicities; for I know I may do very stupid things even in plain matters, unless You keep me out of mischief.

I have only to pray in faith, and You will give me wisdom! Lord, I thank You for that positive and expressive word, "It will be given him." I believe it. You will guide me with Your counsel, and afterwards, receive me to glory.

A TRUSTWORTHY NAME

"I will leave in your midst a meek and humble people,
and they shall trust in the name of the LORD."

~ Zephaniah 3:12

When true religion is ready to die out among the wealthy it finds a home among the poor of this world, rich in faith. The Lord has even now His faithful remnant. Am I one of them?

Perhaps it is because men are afflicted and poor that they learn to trust in the name of the Lord. He whose own name is good for nothing in his own esteem, acts wisely to rest in another name, the name of Jehovah. Little as the world thinks of poor people, they bring untold blessings, for they are the conserving salt that keeps in check the corruption in the world.

Again the question: am I one of them? Do I trust in the Lord? Jesus reveals the name, the character, the person of God: am I trusting in Him? If so, I am left in this world for a purpose. Lord, help me to fulfill it.

A SHEPHERD SECURES THEM

They shall feed their flocks and lie down,
and no one shall make them afraid.

~ Zephaniah 3:13

Yesterday we thought of the afflicted and poor people whom the Lord left to be a living seed in a dead world. The prophet says of such that they shall not work iniquity nor speak lies.

What then? Would they be destroyed for their lack of weapons, in which the wicked place so much reliance? By no means! They should both feed and rest, and be free from danger.

Sheep are very feeble creatures, and wolves are terrible enemies; yet at this hour, sheep are more numerous than wolves, and the cause of the sheep is always winning, while the cause of the wolves is always declining.

One day flocks of sheep will cover the plains, and not a wolf will be left. The fact is that sheep have a shepherd, and this gives them protection, and peace. Who shall terrify the Lord's flock when He is near?

NO CAUSE TO BLUSH

"Do not fear, for you will not be ashamed."

~ *Isaiah 54:4*

We shall not be ashamed of our *faith*. Critics may assail the Scriptures upon which we ground our belief, but every year the Lord will make it more and more clear that in His Book there is no error, no excess, and no omission. It is no discredit to be a simple believer: the faith that looks alone to Jesus is a crown of honor on any man's head.

We shall not be ashamed of our *hope*. Our Lord will come, and then the days of our mourning shall be ended. How we shall glory in the Lord who first gave us lively hope, and then gave us what we hoped for!

We shall not be ashamed of our *love*. Jesus is altogether lovely, and never shall we have to blush because we yielded our hearts to Him. The lovers of Jesus Christ shall find themselves honored by all holy beings.

DWELLING SAFELY APART

*Then Israel shall dwell in safety, the fountain of
Jacob alone, in a land of grain and new
wine; His heavens shall also drop dew.*

~ Deuteronomy 33:28

The more we dwell alone, the safer shall we be. God
would have His people separate from sinners. A
worldly Christian is spiritually diseased. Those who
compromise with Christ's enemies may be reckoned
with them.

Our safety lies not in making terms with the
enemy, but in dwelling alone with our Best Friend.
If we do this, we shall dwell in safety, despite the
sarcasms and the sneers of the world. We shall be
safe from its influence, unbelief, pride, vanity, and
filthiness.

The Lord brought Abram from Ur of the Chal-
dees, but he stopped halfway. Therefore, Abram had
no blessing till, having set out to go to the land of
Canaan, to the land of Canaan he came. He was safe
alone even in the midst of foes. Lot was not safe in
Sodom though in a circle of friends. Our safety is in
dwelling apart with God.

DIVINE CULTIVATION

"I the LORD do keep it; I will water it every moment:
lest any hurt it, I will keep it night and day."

~ Isaiah 27:3 KJV

When the Lord Himself speaks, the word has a peculiar weight. It is Jehovah Himself who is the keeper of His own vineyard; He does not trust it to any other, but He makes it His own personal care. Are they not well kept whom God Himself keeps?

We are to receive gracious watering not only every day and every hour, but "every moment." How we should grow! How fresh and fruitful every plant should be!

But disturbers come, foxes and boars. Therefore, the Lord Himself is our Guardian, both "night and day." What, then, can harm us? He tends, He waters, He guards; what more do we need?

Twice in this verse the Lord says, "I will." What truth, what power, what love is in this! If He says, "I will," what room is there for doubt? With an "I will" of God, we can face all the hosts of sin, death, and hell.

HE CONSTANTLY ABIDES

The LORD will not forsake His people,
for His great name's sake, because it has
pleased the LORD to make you His people.

~ 1 Samuel 12:22

God's choice of His people is the reason for His abiding by them and not forsaking them. He chose them for His love, and He loves them for His choice. It would dishonor His great name for Him to forsake them; since it would either show that He made an error in His choice or that He was fickle in His love. God's love has this glory, that it never changes; and this glory He will never tarnish.

By all the memories of the Lord's former loving-kindnesses, let us rest assured that He will not forsake us. He, who has gone so far as to make us His people, will not undo the creation of His grace. He has not wrought such wonders for us that He might leave us after all. Our Lord Jesus is no changeable Lover. Having loved His own, He loves them to the end.

HOME BLESSINGS EXTENDED

The LORD bless you out of Zion, and may you see
the good of Jerusalem all the days of your life.

~ Psalm 128:5

This is a promise to the God-fearing man who walks in the ways of holiness. He shall have domestic blessedness; his wife and children shall be a source of great happiness. But then as a member of the church, he desires to see the cause prosper, for he is as much concerned for the Lord's house as for his own. When the Lord builds our house, it is but fitting that we should desire to see the Lord's house built.

You shall get a blessing when you go up to the assemblies of Zion. You shall be instructed, enlivened, and comforted where prayer and praise ascend and testimony is borne to the Great Sacrifice.

Nor shall you alone be profited. The church itself shall prosper, believers shall be multiplied, and their holy work shall be crowned with success. Let us be among those who bring good things to Jerusalem all their days.

POSSESS, NOT ONLY PROFESS

*"Whoever has, to him more will be given,
and he will have abundance."*

~ Matthew 13:12

When the Lord has given to a man much grace, He will give him more. A little faith is a nest egg; more faith will come to it. But then it must not be seeming faith, but real and true.

Blessed be the Lord, when He has once made a beginning, He will continue bestowing the graces of His Spirit, till He who had but little is made to have abundance.

Abundance of grace is a thing to be coveted. It would be delightful to have abundance of skill to serve God, but better to have abundance of faith to trust in the Lord for skill and everything.

Lord, since You have given me a sense of sin, deepen my hatred of evil. Since You have caused me to trust Jesus, raise my faith to full assurance. Since You have made me to love You, cause me to be carried away with love for You!

OUR FIELD OF BATTLE

The Lord your God is He who goes with you,
to fight for you against your enemies, to save you.

~ Deuteronomy 20:4

Our only enemies are the enemies of God. Our fights are not against men, but against spiritual wickedness. We war with the devil and the blasphemy and despair that he brings into the field of battle, as well as with the armies of sin. With these we contend earnestly with spiritual weapons.

God abhors evil and, therefore, He goes with us to fight for us in this crusade. He will save us, and He will give us grace to win the victory. Depend upon it that if we are on God's side, God is on our side. With such an ally the outcome is never doubtful.

Might lies with the Father who is Almighty, with Jesus who has all power in heaven and in earth, and with the Holy Spirit who works His will among men.

Soldiers of Christ, put on your armor. Let not this day pass without striking a blow for Jesus.

GOD HIMSELF SHALL WORK

"Now I will rise," says the LORD;
"Now I will be exalted, now I will lift Myself up."

~ Isaiah 33:10

When the spoilers had made the land as waste as if devoured by locusts, and the warriors who had defended the country sat down and wept, then the Lord came to the rescue. God is exalted in the midst of an afflicted people, for they seek His face and trust Him.

Is it a day of sorrow with us? Let us expect to see the Lord gloried in our deliverance. Are we drawn out in fervent prayer? Do we cry day and night unto Him? Then the time for His grace is near. God will lift up Himself at the right season. He will arise when it will be most for the display of His glory. We wish for His glory more than we long for our own deliverance. Let the Lord be exalted, and our chief desire is obtained.

Lord, may we magnify You because You are a good and great God.

A SOUND HEART

Let my heart be blameless regarding
Your statutes, that I may not be ashamed.

~ *Psalm 119:80*

This inspired prayer contains the assurance that those who keep close to the Word of God shall never have cause to be ashamed of doing so.

See, the prayer is for soundness of heart. A sound creed is good, a sound judgment concerning it is better, but a sound heart toward the truth is best of all. We must love the truth, feel the truth, and obey the truth.

Many will be ashamed in the last great day; they will see their folly and be filled with remorse because of their proud infidelity and willful defiance of the Lord. But he who believed what the Lord taught, and did what the Lord commanded, will stand forth, justified in what he did. Then shall the righteous shine forth as the sun.

Let us pray the prayer of our text, and we may be sure that its promise will be fulfilled to us.

THE LORD IS OUR COMPANION

*Yea, though I walk through the valley of the shadow
of death, I will fear no evil; for You are with me;
Your rod and Your staff, they comfort me.*

~ *Psalm 23:4*

Although many have repeated these words in their last hours with intense delight, they are equally applicable to agonies of spirit in the midst of life.

Some of us, like Paul, die daily through a tendency to gloom of soul. Some of us have traversed the dark and dreadful defile of "the shadow of death" several times, and we can bear witness that the Lord alone enabled us to bear up amid its wild thought, its mysterious horrors, and its terrible depressions.

We have been pressed and oppressed, but yet we have lived, for we have felt the presence of the Great Shepherd and have been confident that His crook would prevent the foe from giving us any deadly wound. Should the present time be one darkened by the raven wings of a great sorrow, let us glorify God by a peaceful trust in Him.

A WOMAN'S WAR

The LORD will sell Sisera into
the hand of a woman.

~ Judges 4:9

Rather an unusual text, but there may be souls in the world that may have faith enough to grasp it. Barak, the man, though called to the war, had little stomach for the fight unless Deborah would go with him, and so the Lord determined to make it a woman's war. By this means He rebuked the slackness of the man, and gained for Himself the more renown, and cast the more shame upon the enemies of His people.

The Lord can still use feeble instruments. Why not me? He may use persons who are not commonly called to great public engagements. Why not you?

The woman who slew the enemy of Israel was just a wife who tarried in her tent. She was no orator, but a woman who milked the cows and made butter. May not the Lord use any one of us to accomplish His purpose?

June 22

HE WITH US, WE WITH HIM

The fear of the LORD prolongs days,
but the years of the wicked will be shortened.

~ *Proverbs 10:27*

There is no doubt about it. The fear of the Lord leads to virtuous habits, and these prevent that waste of life that comes of sin and vice. The holy rest, which springs out of faith in the Lord Jesus, also greatly helps a man when he is ill. Every physician rejoices to have a patient whose mind is fully at ease. Worry kills, but confidence in God is like healing medicine.

We have therefore all the arrangements for long life; if it be really for our good, we shall see a good old age. Let us not be overcome with sudden expectation of death the moment we have a finger ache.

And what if we should soon be called to the higher sphere? Certainly there would be nothing to deplore in such a summons, but everything to rejoice in.

The truest lengthening of life is to live while we live, wasting no time, but using every hour for the highest ends. So be it this day.

THE ENEMY FRUSTRATED

*Therefore thus says the LORD concerning the king
of Assyria: "He shall not come into this city, nor
shoot an arrow there, nor come before it with
shield, nor build a siege mound against it."*

~ *2 Kings 19:32*

Although Sennacherib boasted loudly, he could not carry out his threats against the city. The Lord is able to stop the enemies of His people in the very act. When the lion has the lamb between his jaws, the great Shepherd of the sheep can rob him of his prey. Our extremity only provides an opportunity for a grander display of divine power and wisdom.

In the case before us, the terrible foe did not put in an appearance before the city that he thirsted to destroy. No arrow could he shoot over the walls, no shields could he put to work to batter down the castles, and no mounds could he cast up to shut in the inhabitants. Perhaps in our case also, the Lord will prevent our adversaries from doing us the least harm. Let us trust in the Lord and keep His way, and He will take care of us.

THE LORD'S "MUCH MORE"

Amaziah said to the man of God, "But what shall
we do about the hundred talents which I have given
to the troops of Israel?" And the man of God answered,
"The LORD is able to give you much more than this."

~ *2 Chronicles 25:9*

The Lord can give you much more than you are likely to lose. The king of Judah had hired an army from Israel, and he was commanded to send home the fighting men because the Lord was not with them. He was willing to send away the host, only he grudged paying the hundred talents for nothing. Oh, for shame! If the Lord will give the victory without the hirelings, surely it was a good bargain to pay their wages and to be rid of them.

Be willing to lose money for conscience's sake, for peace's sake, for Christ's sake. Rest assured that losses for the Lord are not losses. Even in this life they are more than recompensed. As to our immortal life, what we lose for Jesus is invested in heaven. Fret not at apparent disaster but listen to the whisper, "The LORD is able to give you much more than this."

A STAIRCASE TO HEAVEN

He said to him, "Most assuredly, I say to you,
hereafter you shall see heaven open, and the angels
of God ascending and descending upon the Son of Man."

~ John 1:51

Yes, to our faith this sight is plain even today. Jesus Himself has opened heaven to all believers. We gaze into the place of mystery and glory, for He has revealed it to us.

Now we see the explanation of Jacob's ladder. Between earth and heaven, there is a holy commerce: prayer ascends, and answers come down by the way of Jesus, the Mediator. In Him a stairway of light now furnishes a clear passage to the throne of the Most High. Let us use it, and send up by it the messengers of our prayers.

We shall live the angelic life ourselves if we run up to heaven in intercession, and lay hold upon the blessings of the covenant, and then descend again to scatter those gifts among the sons of men.

This is Your promise, O Lord Jesus; let us joyfully see it fulfilled.

IT WILL NOT BE LONG

You also be patient. Establish your hearts,
for the coming of the Lord is at hand.

~ James 5:8

Among the last words of the Apocalypse we read, "The Spirit and the bride say, 'Come!' to which the heavenly Bridegroom answers, 'Surely I come quickly.'"

Love longs for the glorious appearing of the Lord, and enjoys this sweet promise, "The coming of the Lord is at hand." We look out with hope through this window.

This sacred "window of agate" lets in a flood of light upon the present and puts us into fine condition for immediate work or suffering. Are we tried? Are we growing weary because we do not see the harvest of our seed-sowing? This glorious truth cries to us, "Be patient." Before long the Lord will be here, so establish your hearts. Be firm, be constant, abounding in the work of the Lord. Soon will you hear the trumpets that announce the coming of your King. Hold the fort, for He is coming; He may appear this very day.

THANK HIM AND DWELL ACCEPTABLY

Surely the righteous shall give thanks to Your name;
the upright shall dwell in Your presence.

~ Psalm 140:13

May my heart be upright, and may I always be able to bless the name of the Lord! He is so good to those that are good. Perhaps, for a moment, the righteous are staggered when their integrity results in severe trial; but the day shall come when they shall bless their God that they did not yield to evil or adopt a shifty policy. In the long run, true men will thank God for leading them by a right way.

What a promise is implied in this second clause, "The upright shall dwell in Your presence!" They shall stand accepted where others appear only to be condemned. They shall be favored ones upon whom Jehovah smiles and with whom He graciously communes.

Lord, I covet this high honor, this precious privilege. Make me in all things upright, that I may today, and every day, stand in Your heavenly presence.

ONE LOOK FROM THE LORD!

The LORD turned to him and said, "Go in this might
of yours, and you shall save Israel from the hand
of the Midianites. Have I not sent you?"

~ *Judges 6:14*

What a look was that which the Lord gave to Gideon! He looked him out of his discouragement into a holy bravery. Lord, look on me this day!

Jehovah spoke to Gideon, "Go." He must not hesitate. Gideon might have answered, "What, go in all this weakness?" But the Lord said, "Go in this might of yours." The Lord had looked might into him, and he had now nothing to do but to use it and save Israel by smiting the Midianites. Maybe the Lord has more to do by me than I ever dreamed of. If He has looked upon me, He has made me strong.

What a question is that which the Lord puts to me, even as He put it to Gideon! "Have not I sent you?" Yes, Lord, You have sent me and I will go in strength. At Your command I go; and You will conquer.

INVITATION TO PRAY

"Call to Me, and I will answer you, and show you great and mighty things, which you do not know."

~ Jeremiah 33:3

God encourages us to pray. In this verse Jehovah distinctly promises to answer the prayer of His servant. He that made the ear, shall He not hear? He that gave parents a love to their children, will He not listen to the cries of His own sons and daughters?

God will answer His pleading people in their anguish. He has wonders in store for them. What they have never seen, heard of, or dreamed of, He will do for them.

He will invent new blessings if needful. He will ransack sea and land to feed them: He will send every angel out of heaven to comfort them, if their distress requires it. He will astound us with His grace. All He asks of us is that we will call upon Him. Let us cheerfully render Him our prayers at once.

June 30

BACK, THEN FORWARD

*"Nevertheless I will remember My covenant with you
in the days of your youth, and I will establish
an everlasting covenant with you."*

~ *Ezekiel 16:60*

Notwithstanding our sins, the Lord is still faithful in His love to us.

He looks back. See how He remembers those early days of ours when He took us into covenant with Himself, and we gave ourselves over to Him. He rather looks to His covenant with us than to our covenant with Him. How gracious is the Lord to look back in love!

He looks forward also. He is resolved that the covenant shall not fail. If we do not stand to it, He does. He solemnly declares, "I will establish an everlasting covenant with you." He has no mind to draw back from His promises. Blessed be His name! He rests in His covenant engagements. "He remains faithful; He cannot deny Himself" (2 Tim. 2:13).

O Lord, lay this precious word upon my heart, and help me to feed upon it all this day!

July

GOD WITH US

God will be with you.

~ *Genesis 48:21*

When Jacob's hour came to depart from this world he assured his son, "God will be with you." When our dearest relations or friends are called home by death, we must console ourselves that the Lord is not departed from us, but abides with us forever.

If God be with us, we are in ennobling company and have all-sufficient strength, for nothing is too hard for the Lord. If God be with us, we are always safe, for none can harm those who walk under His shadow. What joy is here! Not only is God with us, but He will be with us. The very name of Jesus is Immanuel – God with us.

Let us be diligent and joyously hopeful. Our cause must prosper; the truth must win, for the Lord is with those who are with Him.

All this day, may this sweet word be enjoyed by every believer. No greater happiness is possible.

REFRESHING SLEEP

He gives His beloved sleep.

~ *Psalm 127:2*

Ours is not a life of anxiety but of happy faith. Our Father will supply the wants of His children, and He knows what we need before we ask Him. If we have learned to rely upon Him then we shall not lie awake with fear gnawing at us; but we shall leave our care with the Lord, and He will give us refreshing sleep.

To be the Lord's beloved is the highest possible honor. He who has it may feel that ambition itself could desire no more, and therefore every selfish wish may fall asleep. What more is there than God's love? Rest then, for you have all things.

Jesus is our peace, our rest, our all. On His bosom we sleep in peace, both in life and in death.

> Sprinkled afresh with pardoning blood,
> I lay me down to rest
> As in the embraces of my God,
> Or on my Savior's breast.

A GUIDE ALL THE WAY

He will be our guide even to death.

~ Psalm 48:14

We need a guide. Often we are willing to do right, but we do not know which road to follow.

The Lord promises to serve as our guide. He knows the way and will pilot us till we reach our journey's end. Surely we do not desire more infallible direction. Let us place ourselves absolutely under His guidance and we shall never miss our way. If we follow His law, we shall not miss the right road of life, provided we lean upon Him every step we take.

Our comfort is that, as He is our God forever, He will never cease to be with us as our guide. "Even to death" will He lead us.

This promise of divine guidance involves lifelong security: salvation at once, guidance unto our last hour, and then endless blessedness. This day let us look up for guidance before we trust ourselves out of doors.

THE WORD, NECESSARY FOOD

"Man shall not live by bread alone, but by every word that proceeds from the mouth of God."

~ Matthew 4:4

If God so willed it we could live without bread, even as Jesus did for forty days; but we could not live without His Word. By that Word we were created, and by it alone can we be kept in being. Bread is a second cause; the Lord Himself is the first source of our sustenance. Let us not be too eager after the visible, but let us look to the invisible God.

We must have the Word of the Lord. With this alone we can withstand the devil. Our souls need food and there is none for them outside of the Word of the Lord.

All the books and all the preachers in the world cannot furnish us a single meal: it is only the Word from the mouth of God that can fill the mouth of a believer. Lord, evermore give us this bread. We prize it above all.

COMPLETE DELIVERANCE

"I will deliver you in that day," says the LORD,
*"and you shall not be given into the hand
of the men of whom you are afraid."*

~ *Jeremiah 39:17*

When the Lord's faithful ones are suffering for Him, they shall have sweet messages of love from Himself. Ebed-Melech was only a despised Ethiopian, but he was kind to Jeremiah, and so the Lord sent him this special promise. Let us be ever mindful of God's persecuted servants, and He will reward us.

Ebed-Melech was to be delivered from the men whose vengeance he feared. He was a humble black man, but Jehovah would take care of him. Thousands were slain by the Chaldeans, but this lowly servant could not be hurt. We, too, may be fearful of ones who are bitter against us; but if we have been faithful to the Lord's cause in the hour of persecution, He will be faithful to us.

No cup of cold water given to a despised prophet of God shall be without its reward; and if we stand up for Jesus, Jesus will stand up for us.

HIS LOVE, HIS GIFT, HIS SON

"For God so loved the world that He gave His only begotten Son, that whoever believes in Him should not perish but have everlasting life."

~ *John 3:16*

Of all the stars in the sky, the pole star is the most useful to the mariner. This text is a pole star, guiding souls to salvation. Several words in it shine with peculiar brilliance.

Here we have God's love, with a "so" to it, which marks its measureless greatness. Then we have God's gift in all its freeness and greatness. This also is God's Son, that unique and priceless gift of a love that could never fully show itself till heaven's Only-begotten had been sent to live and die for men.

Then there is the simple requirement of believing, which graciously points to a way of salvation. This is backed by a wide description, "whoever believes in Him." Then comes the great promise, that believers in Jesus shall not perish, but have everlasting life. This is cheering to all. We believe in the Lord Jesus, and we have eternal life.

A MOUNTAIN CHOIR

*Sing, O heavens! Be joyful, O earth! And break out
in singing, O mountains! For the Lord has comforted
His people, and will have mercy on His afflicted.*

~ Isaiah 49:13

So sweet are the comforts of the Lord that not only
the saints themselves may sing of them, but even
the heavens and the earth take up the song. It takes
something to make a mountain sing; and yet the
prophet summons quite a choir of them. May we not
also make mountains of difficulty, trial, and labor
become occasions for praise unto our God? "Break
out in singing, O mountains!"

This word of promise, that our God will have
mercy upon His afflicted, has a whole peal of bells
connected with it. Hear their music, "Sing!" "Be joyful!" "Break out in singing." The Lord would have
His people happy because of His unfailing love. He
would not have us sad and doubtful. He cannot fail
us: why should we sigh or sulk as if He would?

AN ANGEL ENCAMPMENT

*The angel of the LORD encamps all around
those who fear Him, and delivers them.*

~ *Psalm 34:7*

We cannot see the angels, but it is enough that they can see us. There is one great Angel of the Covenant whose eye is always upon us, both day and night. He has a host of holy ones under Him, and He causes these to be watchers over His saints and to guard them from all ill. If devils do us mischief, shining ones do us service.

Note that the Lord of angels does not come and go, and pay us transient visits, but He and His armies encamp around us. Sentineled by the messengers of God, we shall not be surprised by sudden assaults, or swallowed up by overwhelming forces.

Deliverance is promised in this verse, deliverance by the great Captain of our salvation. That deliverance we shall obtain again and again until our warfare is accomplished and we exchange the field of conflict for the home of rest.

FAITHFUL AND USEFUL

My eyes shall be on the faithful of the land,
that they may dwell with Me; he who walks
in a perfect way, he shall serve Me.

~ *Psalm 101:6*

If David spoke thus, we may be sure that the Son of David will be of the same mind. Jesus looks out for faithful men, and He fixes His eyes upon them, to observe them, to bring them forward, to encourage them, and to reward them. Let no true-hearted man think that he is overlooked; the King Himself has His eye upon him.

There are two results of this royal notice. First we read, "that they may dwell with Me." Jesus sets the faithful in His palace; He makes them His companions; He delights in their society. We must be true to our Lord, and He will then manifest Himself to us.

Next, He says of the sincere man, "he shall serve Me." Jesus will use for His own glory those who are faithful to Himself and His Word. These shall be in His royal retinue, the honored servants of His Majesty. Communion and usefulness are the wages of faithfulness.

LOVE THE CHURCH

You will arise and have mercy on Zion;
for the time to favor her, yes, the set time,
has come. For Your servants take pleasure
in her stones, and show favor to her dust.

~ Psalm 102:13-14

Yes, our prayers for the church will be heard. The set time is come. We are bound in heart to all the people of God, and can truly say,

> There's not a lamb in all Thy flock
> I would disdain to feed;
> There's not a foe before whose face
> I'd fear Thy cause to plead.

If this is the general feeling, we shall soon enjoy times of refreshing from the Lord. Our assemblies will be filled, saints will be revived, and sinners will be converted. We are called upon to expect it. Let us love every stone of our Zion, even though it may be fallen down. Let us treasure up the least truth, the least believer. When we favor Zion, God is about to favor her. When we take pleasure in the Lord's work, the Lord Himself will take pleasure in it.

NEVER SEPARATED FROM GOD

*"Whoever lives and believes in Me shall never die.
Do you believe this?"*

~ *John 11:26*

Yes, Lord, we believe it; we shall never die. Our soul may be separated from our body, but our soul shall never be separated from God, which is the true death. We believe this most assuredly, for who shall separate us from the love of God? We are members of the Body of Christ; will Christ lose parts of His body? We are married to Jesus; will He be bereaved and widowed? It is not possible.

There is a life within us that is not capable of being divided from God. The Holy Spirit dwells within us, and how then can we die? The reward of righteousness is life everlasting; therefore we can claim the very highest reward.

Living and believing, we believe that we shall live and enjoy. Therefore we press forward with full assurance that our life is secure in our living Head.

WHOM, WHEN, HOW TO DELIVER

The Lord knows how to deliver the godly out of temptations and to reserve the unjust under punishment for the day of judgment.

~ 2 Peter 2:9

The godly are tempted and tried, but they are always delivered out of their trials – not by chance, or by secondary agencies, but by the Lord Himself. He personally undertakes the office of delivering those who trust Him.

Sometimes their way seems to be a labyrinth, and they cannot imagine how they will escape. But the Lord knows whom to deliver, when to deliver, and how to deliver. He delivers in the way that is most beneficial to the godly, most crushing to the tempter, and most glorifying to Himself.

We may leave the "how" with the Lord and be content to rejoice in the fact that He will, in some way or other, bring His own people through all the dangers, trials, and temptations of this mortal life.

IMPLICIT TRUST

*"I will surely deliver you, and you shall not fall
by the sword; but your life shall be as a prize to you,
because you have put your trust in Me," says the LORD.*

~ *Jeremiah 39:18*

Behold the protecting power of trust in God. The great men of Jerusalem fell by the sword, but poor Ebed-Melech was secure, for his confidence was in Jehovah. Where else should a man trust but in his Maker? No one ever did trust in the Lord in vain, and no one ever shall.

"I will surely deliver you." Mark the divine *surely*. Under His sacred wing there is safety, even when every danger is abroad. Can we accept this promise as sure? Then in our present emergency we shall find that it stands fast.

We hope to be delivered because we have friends, or because we are prudent, or because we can see hopeful signs; but none of these things are one-half so good as God's simple "because you have put your trust in Me." Try this way and you will keep to it all your life. It is as sweet as it is sure.

BURDENS CAST ON HIM

Cast your burden on the LORD, and He shall sustain you;
He shall never permit the righteous to be moved.

~ *Psalm 55:22*

It is a heavy burden; give it to God. It is your burden now, and it crushes you; but when the Lord takes it, He will make nothing of it. If you are called to bear it, "He shall sustain you." You will be so upheld under it that the burden will be a blessing. Bring the Lord into the matter, and you will stand upright under that which in itself would bow you down.

What about the present moment? Are you going forth to this day's trial alone? Are your poor shoulders again to be galled with the oppressive load? Be not so foolish. Tell the Lord about your grief, and leave it with Him.

Don't cast your burden down and then take it up again; but roll it on the Lord and leave it there. Then you will walk as a joyful and unburdened believer, singing the praises of the great Burden-bearer.

THE MOURNER COMFORTED

"Blessed are those who mourn,
for they shall be comforted."

~ *Matthew 5:4*

By the valley of weeping we come to Zion. One would have thought mourning and being blessed were in opposition, but the infinitely wise Savior puts them together in this beatitude. Mourning for sin – our own sins, and the sins of others – is the Lord's seal set upon His faithful ones. By holy mourning we receive the best of our blessings. Not only shall the mourner be blessed at some future day, but Christ pronounces him blessed even now.

The Holy Spirit will comfort those hearts that mourn for sin. They shall be comforted by the application of the blood of Jesus, and by the cleansing power of the Holy Ghost.

They shall be comforted with the expectation that soon they shall be taken up to dwell forever in the glorious presence of their Lord.

A WORD TO THE LAME

"I will save the lame."

~ *Zephaniah 3:19*

There are plenty of people who are lame in their spirit. They are on the right road, and exceedingly anxious to run in it with diligence; but they are lame and make a sorry walk of it.

On the heavenly road there are many cripples. The Lord can never make good soldiers of people like this. Yet, He will save us. In saving us, He will greatly glorify Himself. Everybody will ask how came this lame person to run the race and win the crown? And then praise will all be given to the Almighty.

Lord, though I halt in faith, in prayer, in praise, in service, and in patience, save me! Lord, gather up by Your grace the slowest of Your pilgrims, even me. He has said that it shall be so. Therefore, like Jacob, prevailing in prayer, I go forward though my sinew be shrunk.

VALIANT FOR TRUTH

*"The people that do know their God
shall be strong, and do exploits."*

~ Daniel 11:32 KJV

"The LORD is a man of war" (Exod. 15:3). Those who enlist under His banner shall have a Commander who will train them for conflict and give them both vigor and valor. The times of which Daniel wrote were of the very worst kind, and then it was promised that the people of God would come out in their best colors: they would be strong and stout to confront the powerful adversary.

Oh, that we may know our God – His power, His faithfulness, His immutable love – and so may be ready to risk everything on His behalf. He is One whose character excites our enthusiasm and makes us willing to live and to die for Him.

If we dwell with Him we shall catch the heroic spirit, and to us a world of enemies will be but as the drop of a bucket. Be valiant for truth in this day of falsehood.

WILDERNESS COMMUNION

*"I will allure her, bring her into
the wilderness, and speak comfort to her."*

~ Hosea 2:14

Do we not remember when the Lover of our souls first cast a spell upon us and charmed us away from the fascinations of the world? He will do this again and again whenever He sees us likely to be ensnared by evil.

He promises to draw us apart, for there He can best deal with us. This separated place is not to be a paradise, but a wilderness, since in such a place there will be nothing to take our attention from our God. In the deserts of affliction, the presence of the Lord becomes everything to us, and we prize His company beyond any value that we set upon it when we sat in the society of our fellows.

When thus allured and secluded, the Lord speaks to our hearts. Allured by love, separated by trial, and comforted by the Spirit of truth, may we know the Lord and sing for joy!

HEAVY DUTY SHOES

Your sandals shall be iron and bronze;
as your days, so shall your strength be.

~ Deuteronomy 33:25

Here are two things provided for the pilgrim: shoes and strength.

The shoes: We shall not go barefoot; this would not be suitable for princes of the royal blood. Our shoes shall have soles of durable metal, which will not wear out even if the journey be long and difficult. We shall have protection proportionate to the necessities of the road and the battle. So let us march boldly on, fearing no harm even though we tread on serpents, or set our foot upon the dragon himself.

The strength: It shall be continued as long as our days shall continue, and it shall be proportioned to the stress and burden of those days. This day we may look for trial and for work, which will require energy, but we may just as confidently look for equal strength. Let us rise to the holy boldness, which it is calculated to create within the believing heart.

LOOKING FOR HIM

*To those who eagerly wait for Him He will appear
a second time, apart from sin, for salvation.*

~ Hebrews 9:28

This is our hope. He to whom we have already looked as coming once to bear the sins of many will have another manifestation to the sons of men; this is a happy prospect in itself. But that second appearing has certain peculiar marks that glorify it exceedingly.

Our Lord will have ended the business of sin. He has so taken it away from His people, and so effectually borne its penalty that He will have nothing to do with it at His Second Coming. He will present no sin offering, for He will have utterly put sin away.

Our Lord will then complete the salvation of His people. They will be finally and perfectly saved, and will in every respect enjoy the fullness of that salvation.

Our Lord thus appears only to those who look for Him. We must first look to Him, and then look for Him; and in both cases our look shall be life.

SHINE AS MANY STARS

*Those who are wise shall shine like the brightness
of the firmament, and those who turn many to
righteousness like the stars forever and ever.*

~ Daniel 12:3

To be wise is a noble thing in itself: in this place it refers to a divine wisdom, which only the Lord Himself can bestow. May I be so divinely taught that I may carry into practice heavenly truth and live in the light of it! Is my life a wise one? Am I seeking that which I ought to seek? Am I living as I shall wish I had lived when I come to die? Only such wisdom can secure for me eternal brightness as of yonder sunlit skies.

To be a winner of souls is a glorious attainment. I had need be wise if I am to turn even one to righteousness, much more if I am to turn many. Oh for the knowledge of God, of men, of the Word, and of Christ, which will enable me to convert my fellow men! This will make me a star, shining forever and ever.

AN ETERNAL PLEDGE

"I will betroth you to Me forever; yes, I will betroth you to Me in righteousness and justice, in lovingkindness and mercy; I will betroth you to Me in faithfulness, and you shall know the Lord.*"*

~ Hosea 2:19-20

Betrothment to the Lord! And it is forever – He will never break His engagement, much less propose divorce against a soul joined to Himself in marriage bonds.

Righteousness comes in to make the covenant legal; none can forbid these lawful banns. Judgment sanctions the alliance with its decree: none can see folly or error in the match. Loving-kindness warrants that this is a love union, for without love betrothal is bondage, and not blessedness. Meanwhile, mercy smiles, and even sings; she multiplies herself into "mercies," because of the abounding grace of this holy union. Faithfulness is the registrar and records the marriage, and the Holy Spirit says "Amen" to it, as He promises to teach the betrothal heart all the sacred knowledge needful for its high destiny. What a promise!

ABSOLUTELY NO REMEMBRANCE

*"Their sins and their lawless deeds
I will remember no more."*

~ Hebrews 10:17

The Lord treats His people as if they had never sinned. Their sins are erased from His memory. What grace!

We may rejoice in Him without fear that He will be provoked to anger against us because of our iniquities. He puts us among the children; He accepts us as righteous; He takes delight in us as if we were perfectly holy. He even puts us into places of trust and makes us guardians of His honor, trustees of the crown jewels, stewards of the gospel.

He counts us worthy; this is the highest and most special proof that He does not remember our sins. Even when we forgive an enemy, we are very slow to trust him; we judge it to be imprudent so to do. But the Lord forgets our sins and treats us as if we had never erred. What a promise is this! Believe it and be happy.

PERFECT PURITY

*"He who overcomes shall be
clothed in white garments."*

~ Revelation 3:5

Warrior of the cross, fight on! Never rest till the victory is complete, for your eternal reward will prove worthy of a life of warfare.

See, here is perfect purity! Perfect holiness is the prize of our high calling, let us not miss it.

See, here is joy! You shall be clothed with gladness and be made bright with rejoicing. Painful struggles shall end in peace of conscience, and joy in the Lord.

See, here is victory! You will triumph and shall be treated as a conqueror.

See, here is priestly array! You shall stand before the Lord in such garments as the sons of Aaron wore; you shall offer the sacrifices of thanksgiving and draw near unto the Lord with the incense of praise.

Who would not fight for a Lord who gives such large honors to the very least of His faithful servants?

NOTHING TO ALARM US

*"Go your way till the end; for you shall rest, and
will arise to your inheritance at the end of the days."*

~ Daniel 12:13

We cannot understand all the prophecies, but we regard them with pleasure and not with dismay. There can be nothing in the Father's decree that should alarm His child. Though the earth be burned up, no smell of fire shall come upon the chosen. The Lord Jehovah will preserve His own.

Calmly resolute in duty, brave in conflict, patient in suffering, let us go our way, keeping to our road, neither swerving from it, nor loitering in it.

Rest will be ours. All other things swing to and fro, but our foundation stands sure. God rests in His love, and, therefore, we rest in it: Our peace is, and ever shall be, like a river.

The God of Daniel will give a worthy portion to all who dare to be decided for truth and holiness as Daniel was. No den of lions shall deprive us of our sure inheritance.

A CHANGE OF NAME

"It shall be, in that day," says the LORD,
"That you will call Me 'My Husband,'
and no longer call Me 'My Master,'
for I will take from her mouth
the names of the Baals, and they shall be
remembered by their name no more."

~ Hosea 2:16-17

That day has come. We view our God no more as Baal, our tyrant lord, but as our Ishi, our beloved Husband, our Lord in love. We do not revere Him less, but we love Him more. We do not serve Him less obediently, but we serve Him for a higher and more endearing reason. We no longer tremble under His lash, but rejoice in His love.

Is it so with you, dear reader? Has grace cast out fear and implanted love? How happy are we in such an experience! Now we call the Lord's Day a delight, and worship is never a weariness. Prayer is now a privilege, and praise is a holiday. To obey is heaven; to give to the cause of God is a banquet. Thus have all things become new. Our mouth is filled with singing, and our heart with music. Blessed be our heavenly Ishi forever.

MORE THAN MERE WORDS

"I will give you the sure mercies of David."

~ *Acts 13:34*

Nothing of man is sure, but everything of God is so. Especially His covenant mercies.

The Lord does not speak mere words: there is substance and truth in every one of His promises. We are sure that the Lord will bestow promised mercies on all His covenanted ones. They shall come in due course to all the chosen of the Lord, from the least of them unto the greatest of them.

We are sure that the Lord will continue His mercies to His own people. He does not give and take. That which we have not yet received is as sure as that which has already come; therefore, let us wait before the Lord and be still. There is no justifiable reason for the least doubt. God's love, and word, and faithfulness are sure. Many things are questionable, but of the Lord we sing:

> For His mercies shall endure
> Ever faithful, ever sure.

BOW DOWN TO BE LIFTED UP

Therefore humble yourselves under the mighty hand
of God, that He may exalt you in due time.

~ 1 Peter 5:6

If we will bow down, the Lord will lift us up. Humility leads to honor; submission leads to exaltation. That same hand of God that presses us down is waiting to raise us up when we are prepared to bear the blessing. He who humbles himself under God shall not fail to be enriched, uplifted, sustained, and comforted by Him.

Yet there is a time for the Lord's working. We ought now to humble ourselves, and we are bound to keep on doing so whether the Lord lays His afflicting hand upon us or not.

As for the Lord's exaltation of us, that can only come "in due time," and God is the best judge of that day and hour. Do we cry out impatiently for the blessing? Would we wish for untimely honor? Surely we are not truly humbled, or we should wait with quiet submission. So let us do so.

HE DESTROYS OUR ENEMY

The LORD has cast out your enemy.

~ Zephaniah 3:15

What a casting out! Satan has lost his throne in our nature – our Lord has destroyed his power over us. He may worry us, but he cannot claim us as his own. His bonds are no longer upon our spirits: Jesus has made us free.

As a tempter, the evil spirit still assails us and insinuates himself into our minds, but then also is he cast out as to his former preeminence. He wriggles about like a serpent, but he cannot rule like a sovereign. He hurls in blasphemous thoughts when he has opportunity, but what a relief it is when he is told to be quiet and is made to slink off like a whipped dog!

Lord, do this for any who are at this time worried and wearied by his barkings. Cast out their enemy, and be glorious in their eyes.

PROMISE OF FUTURE MEETING

*"I will see you again and
your heart will rejoice."*

~ John 16:22

Surely God will come a second time. Oh for that joyous return!

Our gracious Lord has many "agains" in His dealings with us. He gave us pardon and still, again and again He forgives us. When our faith grows a little dim, He comes to us again and again saying, "Peace be unto you."

All our past mercies are tokens of future mercies. If Jesus has been with us, He will see us again. Look upon no former favor as dead and buried, but regard it as a seed sown, which will grow and push its head up from the dust, and cry, "I will see you again."

Are times dark because Jesus is not with us as He used to be? Let us pluck up courage, for He will not be long away. Let us be joyous, since He says to us even now, "I will see you again."

AN APPEAL FOR DELIVERANCE

"Call upon Me in the day of trouble;
I will deliver you, and you shall glorify Me."

~ *Psalm 50:15*

This is a promise indeed!

Here is an urgent occasion: "the day of trouble." It is dark at noon on such a day, and every hour seems blacker than the one that came before it.

Here is advice: "Call upon Me." This should be our constant habit all day and every day. The Lord invites us to lay our case before Him, and surely we will not hesitate to do so.

Here is reassuring encouragement: "I will deliver you." Whatever the trouble may be, the Lord makes no exceptions, but promises full deliverance. We believe it, and the Lord honors faith.

Here is an ultimate result: "You will glorify Me." When He has delivered us, we will loudly praise Him; and as He is sure to do it, let us begin to glorify Him at once.

August

COVENANT REACHES CHILDREN

*"I will establish My covenant between Me and you
and your descendants after you in their generations,
for an everlasting covenant, to be God
to you and your descendants after you."*

~ *Genesis 17:7*

Lord, You have made a covenant with me, Your servant, in Christ Jesus; and now, I implore You, let my children be included in its gracious provisions. Permit me to believe this promise as made to me as well as to Abraham. I know that my children are born in sin; therefore, I ask nothing on the ground of their birth, for well I know that "that which is born of the flesh is flesh," (John 3:6) and nothing more. Lord, make them to be born under Your covenant of grace by Your Holy Spirit!

I pray for my descendants throughout all generations. Be their God as You are mine. My highest honor is that You have permitted me to serve You; may my offspring serve You in all years to come.

Let not one of those who fear Your name be tried with a godless household.

SPEAK WHAT HE TEACHES

*"Now therefore, go, and I will be with your mouth
and teach you what you shall say."*

~ Exodus 4:12

Many a true servant of the Lord is slow of speech, and when called upon to plead for his Lord, he is in great confusion lest he should spoil a good cause by his bad advocacy. But remember, the Lord made the tongue! Lack of fluency is not so great a lack as it looks. Fewness of words may sometimes be more of a blessing than floods of words.

If God be with our mouths and with our minds, we shall have something better than the sounding brass of eloquence or the tinkling cymbal of persuasion.

Pharaoh had more reason to be afraid of stammering Moses than of the most fluent talker in Egypt, for what he said had power in it; he spoke plagues and deaths. If the Lord be with us in our natural weakness, we shall be strengthened with supernatural power. Therefore, let us speak for Jesus boldly, as we ought to.

THE RIGHT TO HOLY THINGS

*If the priest buys a person with his money,
he may eat it; and one who is born
in his house may eat his food.*

~ *Leviticus 22:11*

Strangers, sojourners, and servants were not to eat of holy things. But two classes were free at the sacred table, those who were *bought* with the priest's money, and those who were *born* into the priest's house. These were the two indisputable proofs of a right to holy things.

Bought. Our great High Priest has bought with a price all those who put their trust in Him. They are His absolute property and "they may eat his food." Because you belong to Christ, you will share with your Lord.

Born. If born in the Priest's house, we take our place with the rest of the family. Regeneration makes us fellow heirs, and of the same body; and, therefore, the peace, joy, and glory, which the Father has given to Christ, Christ has given to us. Redemption and regeneration have given us a double claim to the divine permit of this promise.

HE BLESSES AND KEEPS

The LORD bless you and keep you.

~ Numbers 6:24

What a joy to abide under the divine blessing! This puts a gracious flavor into all things. If we are blessed, then all our possessions and enjoyments are blessed; even our losses and disappointments are blessed! God's blessing is deep, emphatic, and effectual. A man's blessing may begin and end in words, but the blessing of the Lord makes rich and sanctifies.

It is equally a delightful thing to be kept of God: kept by Him, kept near Him, kept in Him: They are kept indeed whom God keeps: they are preserved from evil; they are reserved unto boundless happiness. God's keeping goes with His blessing to establish it and cause it to endure.

May the rich blessing and sure keeping here pronounced come upon every reader who may at this moment be looking at these lines. Please breathe the text to God as a prayer for His servants.

LAW IN THE HEART

The law of his God is in his heart;
none of his steps shall slide.

~ Psalm 37:31

Put the law into the heart, and the whole man is right. This is where the law should be, for in the head it puzzles, on the back it burdens, in the heart it upholds. God with us in covenant makes us eager to obey His will and walk in His commands.

We are here guaranteed that obedient-hearted man shall be sustained, he will do that which is right, and he shall do that which is wise. Holy action is always the most prudent, though it may not at the time seem to be so.

The Word of God has never misled a single soul yet; its plain directions to walk humbly, justly, lovingly, and in the fear of the Lord are as much words of wisdom to make our way prosperous as rules of holiness to keep our garments clean. He walks surely who walks righteously.

GO AND TAKE YOUR PROPERTY

Look, the LORD your God has set the land before you;
go up and possess it, as the LORD God
of your fathers has spoken to you;
do not fear or be discouraged.

~ Deuteronomy 1:21

There is a heritage of grace that we ought to be bold enough to win for our possession. All that one believer has gained is free to another. We may be strong in faith, fervent in love, and abundant in labor; there is nothing to prevent it. Let us go up and take possession. The sweetest experience and the brightest grace are as much for us as for any of our brethren. Jehovah has set it before us; no one can deny our right.

The world also lies before us to be conquered for the Lord Jesus. We are not to leave any country or corner of it unsubdued. We have only to summon courage enough to go forward, and we shall win dark homes and hard hearts for Jesus. No spot is too benighted, no person so profane as to be beyond the power of grace. Cowardice, be gone! Faith marches to the conquest.

RULES FOR PROSPERITY

"Only be strong and very courageous, that you may observe to do according to all the law which Moses My servant commanded you; do not turn from it to the right hand or to the left, that you may prosper wherever you go."

~ *Joshua 1:7*

Yes, the Lord will be with us in our holy war, but He demands that we strictly follow His rules. Our victories will depend upon our obeying Him *with all our heart*, throwing strength and courage into the actions of our faith. If we are half-hearted, we cannot expect more than half a blessing.

We must obey the Lord *with care and thoughtfulness*. "Observe to do" is the phrase used, and it is full of meaning. This is referred to every part of the divine will; we must obey *with universal readiness*. Our rule of conduct is "according to all the law." We may not pick and choose, but we must take the Lord's commands as they come, one and all.

In all this we must go on *with exactness and constancy*. With such obedience there will come spiritual prosperity.

CONFIDENCE NOT MISPLACED

"The Lord GOD will help Me."

~ Isaiah 50:7

These are in prophecy the words of Messiah in the day of His obedience unto death. He was confident in divine support and trusted in Jehovah.

My sorrows are as small dust compared with the Lord's! Can I doubt that the Lord God will help me? As the representative of sinful men, as their substitute and sacrifice, it was needful that the Father should leave Jesus and cause Him to come under desertion of soul. Even in such a case Jesus still relied upon God, so cannot then you?

In this day's labors or trials say, "The Lord God will help me." Go forth boldly. If God helps, who can hinder? If you are sure of His aid, what can be too heavy for you?

Begin the day joyously, and let no shade of doubt come between you and the eternal sunshine.

PRUNING FOR FRUITFULNESS

*"Every branch in Me that does not bear fruit
He takes away; and every branch that bears fruit
He prunes, that it may bear more fruit."*

~ John 15:2

This is a precious promise to one who lives for fruitfulness. But must the fruitful bough be pruned? Yes, for much of our Lord's purging work is done by means of afflictions of one kind or another.

It is not the evil but the good who have the promise of tribulation in this life. But then, the end makes more than full amends for the painful nature of the means. If we may bring forth more fruit for our Lord, we will not mind the pruning and the loss of leafage.

The Lord, who has made us fruit bearing, will operate upon us till we reach a far higher degree of fertility. Is not this a great joy? Truly there is more comfort in a promise of fruitfulness than if we had been warranted riches, or health, or honor.

Lord, fulfill Your gracious word to me and cause me to abound in fruit!

HE LOWERS TO RAISE

The LORD makes poor and makes rich;
He brings low and lifts up.

~ 1 Samuel 2:7

All my changes come from Him who never changes. If I had grown rich, I should have seen His hand in it, and I should have praised Him; let me equally see His hand if I am made poor, and let me as heartily praise Him. In any case, the Lord has done it, and it is well.

It seems that Jehovah's way is to lower those whom He means to raise, and to strip those whom He intends to clothe. If I am now enduring the bringing low, I may well rejoice because I see in it the preface to the lifting up. The more we are humbled by grace, the more we shall be exalted in glory.

Lord, You have taken me down of late and made me feel my insignificance and sin. It is not a pleasant experience, but I pray You make it a profitable one to me. Amen.

WAITING, NOT RUNNING

Truly my soul silently waits for God;
from Him comes my salvation.

~ *Psalm 62:1*

Waiting on the Lord. Be this our condition all day and every day – waiting in joyful expectation and prayer. When the soul thus waits, it is in the best and truest condition. We allow no dictation to God, no complaining or distrust of Him, and no seeking others for aid: neither of these would be waiting upon God. God, and God alone, is the expectation of our hearts.

From Him salvation is coming, it is on the road. It will come from Him and from no one else. He shall have all the glory of it for He alone can and will perform it.

Though we see no sign of it as yet, we are satisfied to bide the Lord's will, for we know of His love and faithfulness. He will make sure work of it before long, and we will praise Him at once for the coming mercy.

LIGHT IN DARKNESS

*You are my lamp, O LORD; the LORD
shall enlighten my darkness.*

~ 2 Samuel 22:29

Am I in the light? Then You, Lord, are my lamp.
What a light the presence of God casts on all things!
Lord, I am as happy as an angel when Your love fills
my heart. You are all I desire.

Am I in the dark? Then You, Lord, will lighten
my darkness. Before long things will change. Affairs
may grow more and more dreary; but if it grows so
dark that I cannot see my own hand, still I shall see
the hand of the Lord.

When I cannot find a light within me, or among
my friends, or in the whole world, the Lord – who
said, "Let there be light," and there was light – can say
the same again. He will speak me into the sunshine
yet. The day is already breaking. This sweet text
shines like a morning star. I shall clap my hands for
joy before many hours are passed.

BEFORE AND DURING THE CALL

> *"It shall come to pass that before they call,*
> *I will answer; and while they*
> *are still speaking, I will hear."*
>
> ~ *Isaiah 65:24*

The Lord hears us before we call. Foreseeing our needs and prayers, He so arranges providence that before the need actually arises He has supplied it, before the trial assails us He has armed us against it. What a prayer-answering God we have!

Look at the second clause. Though God be in heaven and we upon earth, when we pray aright we speak into the ear of God. Our gracious Mediator presents our petitions at once, and the great Father hears them and smiles upon them.

Who would not be much in prayer when he knows that he has the ear of the King of kings? This day I will pray in faith, not only believing that I shall be heard, but that I am heard; not only that I shall be answered, but that I have the answer already.

CHASTISEMENT NOT FOREVER

*"I will afflict the descendants of
David because of this, but not forever."*

~ 1 Kings 11:39

In the family of grace there is discipline. Solomon grievously provoked the God of his father; therefore, ten parts out of twelve of the kingdom were rent away and set up as a rival state. This was a sore affliction, and it came from the hand of God as the result of unholy conduct.

The Lord will chasten His beloved servants if they cease to obey His laws. Perhaps at this very hour such chastening is upon us. Let us humbly cry, "O Lord, show me why You contend with me."

What a sweet saving clause is that, "but not forever!" The punishment of sin is everlasting, but the fatherly chastisement of it for a child of God is but for a season. Remember, we are not under law, but under grace. Our present grief is meant to bring us to repentance, that we may not be destroyed with the wicked.

A NAME GUARANTEE

"Whatever you ask in My name, that I will do,
that the Father may be glorified in the Son."

~ *John 14:13*

To ask not only for Jesus' sake, but in His name, as authorized by Him, is a high order of prayer. We would not dare to ask for some things in that blessed name, but when the petition is so clearly right that we dare set the name of Jesus to it, then it must be granted.

Prayer is all the more sure to succeed because it is for the Father's glory. It glorifies His faithfulness, His power, His grace. The granting of prayer, when offered in the name of Jesus, reveals the Father's love to Him, and the honor which He has put upon Him. The glory of Jesus and of the Father are so wrapped up together that the grace which magnifies the one magnifies the other.

Since in this He is glorified, we will pray without ceasing in that dear name in which God and His people have a fellowship of delight.

UNCOVER AND CONFESS SIN

He who covers his sins will not prosper, but whoever confesses and forsakes them will have mercy.

~ Proverbs 28:13

Here is the way of mercy for a sinner. He must cease from the habit of covering sin. This is attempted by falsehood, which denies sin; by hypocrisy, which conceals it; by boasting, which justifies it, and by loud profession, which tries to make amends for it.

The sinner must confess and forsake. Confession must be honestly made to the Lord. We must not throw the fault upon others, or blame circumstances, or plead natural weakness. We must make a clean breast of it and plead guilty. There can be no mercy till this is done.

Furthermore, having owned our fault, we must disown all present and future intent to abide in it. The habit of evil must be quitted, together with all places, companions and pursuits, which might lead us astray. Not for confession, not for reformation, but in connection with them, we find pardon by faith in the blood of Jesus.

WHO HAS THE MAJORITY?

*He answered, "Do not fear, for those who are with
us are more than those who are with them."*

~ 2 Kings 6:16

Horses, chariots and a great host shut up the prophet in Dothan. His servant was alarmed. How could they escape from such a body of armed men? But the prophet had eyes that his servant had not, and he could see a greater host, with far superior weapons, guarding him from all harm. Horses of fire are mightier than horses of flesh, and chariots of fire are preferable to chariots of iron.

The adversaries of truth are many – and truth fares ill at their hands – yet the man of God has no cause for trepidation. God has armies in ambush that will reveal themselves in the hour of need. The forces that are on the side of the good and the true far outweigh the powers of evil.

Therefore, let us keep our spirits up, for we possess a cheering secret that has lifted us above all fear. We are on the winning side.

SEEKERS AND FINDERS

If you seek Him,
He will be found by you.

~ *1 Chronicles 28:9*

We need our God, and He will not deny Himself to any one of us if we seek His face. It is not if you deserve Him or purchase His favor, but merely if you "seek" Him. Those who already know the Lord must go on seeking His face by prayer, diligent service, and holy gratitude. Those who, as yet, have not known Him should at once commence seeking, and never cease till they find Him as their Savior, their Father, and their God.

What strong assurance this promise gives to the seeker! "He who seeks finds" (Matt. 7:8). You, yes you, if you seek your God, shall find Him. When you find Him, you have found life, sanctification, and glory.

Seek the Lord at once. Bend that stiff knee, bend that stiffer neck, and cry out for the living God. In the name of Jesus, seek cleansing and justification. You shall not be refused.

REWARD FOR RIGHTEOUSNESS

So that men will say, "Surely there is a reward for the righteous; surely He is God who judges in the earth."

~ Psalm 58:11

God's judgments in this life are not always clearly to be seen, for in many cases one event happens alike to all. This is the state of probation, not of punishment or reward. Yet at times God works terrible things in righteousness, and even the careless have to own His hand.

Even in this life, righteousness has that kind of reward, which it prefers above all others, namely, the smile of God, which creates a quiet conscience. Sometimes other recompenses follow, but the chief reward of the righteous lies in the hereafter.

Meanwhile, on a large scale, we mark the presence of the great Ruler among the nations. No one can study the history of the rise and fall of empires without perceiving that there is a power which makes for righteousness, and condemns iniquity. Sin shall not go unpunished, and goodness shall not remain unrewarded. The Judge of all the earth must do right.

DELIVERANCE NOT LIMITED

He shall deliver you in six troubles,
yes, in seven no evil shall touch you.

~ *Job 5:19*

The rapid succession of trials is one of the sorest tests of faith. Before we have recovered from one blow it is followed by others, until we are staggered.

Still, the equally quick succession of deliverances is exceedingly cheering. New songs are rung out upon the anvil by the hammer of affliction, till we see in the spiritual world the antitype of "The Harmonious Blacksmith." Our confidence is that, when the Lord makes our trials six, six they will be and no more.

It may be that we have no rest day, for seven troubles come upon us. What then? "In seven no evil shall touch you." Evil may roar at us, its hot breath may distress us, but its little finger cannot be laid upon us.

So we will meet the six or the seven troubles, and leave fear to those who have no Father and no Savior.

NIGHT OF WEEPING, JOYOUS DAY

His anger is but for a moment,
His favor is for life; weeping may endure
for a night, but joy comes in the morning.

~ Psalm 30:5

A moment under our Father's anger seems very long, yet it is but a moment after all. If we grieve His Spirit, we cannot look for His smile; but He is a God ready to pardon. When we faint and are ready to die because of His frown, His favor puts new life into us.

This verse has another note. Our weeping night soon turns into joyous day. He gives a blow or two, and all is over. And the life and the joy, which follow the anger and the weeping, more than make amends for the salutary sorrow.

Come, my heart, begin your hallelujahs! Weep not all through the night, but wipe your eyes in anticipation of the morning. Tears clear the eyes for the sight of God in His grace; and make the vision of His favor more precious. All is well.

WRATH TO GOD'S GLORY

Surely the wrath of man shall praise You;
with the remainder of wrath You shall gird Yourself.

~ Psalm 76:10

Wicked men will be wrathful. If we were of the world, the world would love its own. Our comfort is that the wrath of man shall be made to rebound to the glory of God. When, in their wrath, the wicked crucified the Son of God, they were unwittingly fulfilling the divine purpose, and in a thousand cases the willfulness of the ungodly is doing the same. They think themselves free, but like convicts in chains they are unconsciously working out the decrees of the Almighty.

Nothing will come of their wrath which can do us real harm. Meanwhile, the Lord restrains the more furious wrath of the enemy. He is like a miller who holds back the mass of the water in the stream, and what He does allow to flow, He uses for the turning of His wheel. Let us not sigh, but sing. All is well, however hard the wind blows.

LOVE AND SEEK
TRUE WISDOM

*I love those who love me, and those who
seek me diligently will find me.*

~ *Proverbs 8:17*

Wisdom loves her lovers and seeks her seekers. He is already wise who seeks to be wise, and he has almost found wisdom who diligently seeks her. What is true of wisdom in general is especially true of wisdom embodied in our Lord Jesus. Him we are to love and to seek; and in return, we shall enjoy His love and find Him.

It is never too soon to seek the Lord Jesus. Early seekers make certain finders. We should seek Him early by diligence. Those who find Jesus to their enrichment give their hearts to seeking Him. We must seek Him first, and thus earliest. Above all things, Jesus – Jesus first.

The blessing is that He will be found. Happy men who seek One who, when He is found, remains with them forever, a treasure growingly precious to their hearts and understandings.

GOD ABOVE HUMAN PHILOSOPHY

*It is written: "I will destroy the wisdom of the wise,
and bring to nothing the understanding of the prudent."*

~ 1 Corinthians 1:19

The professedly learned are forever trying to bring to nothing the faith of the humble believer, but they fail in their attempts. Their arguments break down and their theories fall under their own weight. The gospel is not extinct – nor will it be while the Lord lives. If it could have been exterminated, it would have perished from off the earth long ago.

We cannot destroy the wisdom of the wise, nor need we attempt it, for the work is in far better hands. The Lord Himself says, "I will," and He never resolves in vain. We may rest assured that He will not turn aside from it.

What clean work the Lord makes of philosophy and "modern thought" when He puts His hand to it! It is written that so it shall be, and so shall it be. Lord, make short work of it. Amen.

FOOD AND REST

*"I will feed My flock, and I will make
them lie down," says the Lord God.*

~ *Ezekiel 34:15*

Under the divine shepherdy, saints are fed to the full. Theirs is not a windy, unsatisfying mess of mere human thought; but the Lord feeds them upon the solid, substantial truth of divine revelation. Jesus Himself is the true life-sustaining Food of believers.

When filled with holy truth, the mind rests. Those whom Jehovah feeds are at peace. No dog shall worry them, no wolf shall devour them, no restless propensities shall disturb them. They shall lie down and digest the food which they have enjoyed. The doctrines of grace are not only sustaining, but consoling: in them we have the means for building up and lying down.

This day may the Lord cause us to feed in the pastures of the Word and make us to lie down in them. May no folly, and no worry, but meditation and peace mark this day.

HE OF TENDER CONSCIENCE

"I will judge between sheep and sheep."

~ *Ezekiel 34:22*

Some are fat and flourishing, and therefore they are unkind to the feeble. This is a grievous sin and causes much sorrow. The Lord takes note of their proud and unkind deeds, and He is greatly angered by them, for He loves the weak.

Is the reader one of the despised? Is he a mourner in Zion and a marked man because of his tender conscience? Is he judged harshly by others? Let him not resent their conduct; above all let him not push and thrust in return. Let him leave the matter in the Lord's hands. He is the Judge. Why should we wish to intrude upon His office? He will decide much more righteously than we can. His time for judgment is the best, and we need not be in a hurry to hasten it on.

Patience, my soul! Patience! The Lord knows your grief. Your Jesus has pity upon you!

CHOICE MEN

*"I have chosen thee in the
furnace of affliction."*

~ Isaiah 48:10 KJV

It is no mean thing to be chosen of God. So eminent is this privilege, that whatever drawback may be joined to it we very joyfully accept it. We choose the furnace since God chooses us in it.

We are chosen as an afflicted people and not as a prosperous people: chosen not in the palace, but in the furnace. In the furnace beauty is marred, strength is melted, glory is consumed, and yet here eternal love reveals its secrets and declares its choice.

So has it been in our case. In times of severest trial, God has made to us our calling and election plain. We have chosen the Lord to be our God, and He has shown that we are assuredly His chosen.

Therefore, if today the furnace be heated seven times hotter, we will not dread it, for the glorious Son of God will walk with us amid the glowing coals.

OUT OF ANY CIRCUMSTANCE

As for me, I will call upon God,
*and the L*ORD *shall save me.*

~ Psalm 55:16

I must and will pray. What else can I do? What better can I do? Betrayed, forsaken, grieved, baffled, Lord, I will call upon You. I encourage my heart in the Lord, who will bear me through this trial as He has borne me through so many others.

The Lord alone shall save me. I desire no other helper. I will cry to Him evening, morning, and noon, and I will cry to no one else, for He is All-sufficient.

How He will save me I cannot guess, but He will do it. He will do it in the best and surest way. Out of this trouble and all future troubles, the great I AM will bring me as surely as He lives.

This shall be my song all through today. Is it not as a ripe apple from the tree of life? I will feed upon it. How sweet it is to my taste!

PLENTIFUL REFRESHMENT

*"Their souls shall be like
a well-watered garden."*

~ *Jeremiah 31:12*

Oh, to have one's soul under heavenly cultivation; no longer a wilderness, but a garden of the Lord! Walled around by grace, planted by instruction, visited by love, weeded by heavenly discipline, and guarded by divine power, one's favored soul is prepared to yield fruit unto the Lord.

But a garden may become parched for want of water, and then it starts to wither. How soon would this be the case, were the Lord to leave us! A garden without water ceases to be a garden at all: nothing can come to perfection, grow or even live.

But when irrigation is kept up, the result is charming. Oh, to have one's soul watered by the Holy Spirit uniformly, every part of the garden having its own stream. Bringing not only its heat, but its refreshment; each plant receiving just what it needs.

Lord, water me today, and cause me to yield You a full reward.

SOLACE, SECURITY, SATISFACTION

Although my house is not so with God, yet He has made
with me an everlasting covenant, ordered in all things
and secure. For this is all my salvation and all
my desire; will He not make it increase?

~ *2 Samuel 23:5*

These are David's words, but they may be mine today. Here is a sigh: things are not with me as I could wish; there are trials, cares, and sins. These make the pillow hard.

Here is a *solace*, "He has made with me an everlasting covenant." Jehovah has pledged Himself to me and sealed the compact with the blood of Jesus. I am bound to my God, and my God to me.

This brings into prominence a *security*, since this covenant is everlasting and sure. There is nothing to fear from the lapse of time, or the natural uncertainty of things.

David feels *satisfaction*: he wants no more for salvation; he is delivered, and he is delighted. The covenant is all a man can desire.

Turn this day to the Lord Jesus, whom the great Lord has given to be a covenant to the people.

DIVINE, EVER-LIVING, UNCHANGING

"The word of the Lord endures forever."
Now this is the word which by the
gospel was preached to you.

~ *1 Peter 1:25*

All human teaching shall pass away; but we are assured that the Word of the Lord shall endure forever.

We have a *divine gospel*; for what word can endure forever but that which is spoken by the eternal God?

We have an *ever-living gospel*, as full of vitality as when it first came from the lips of God; as strong to convince and convert, console, sustain and sanctify, as ever it was in its first days.

We have an *unchanging gospel*, which is not today green grass and tomorrow dry hay, but always the abiding truth of God. Opinions alter, but truth certified by God can no more change than the God who uttered it.

Here, then, we have a *gospel to rejoice in*. Feed on the Word today, and all the days of your life.

September

ABIDING IN
OBEDIENCE AND LOVE

*"If you keep My commandments,
you will abide in My love."*

~ *John 15:10*

These things cannot be parted – abiding in obedience and abiding in the love of Jesus. We must keep our Lord's command if we would bask in His love.

Conscious enjoyment of our Lord's love is a delicate thing. When we are tender of heart and careful in thought, mouth, and life to honor our Lord Jesus, then we receive tokens of His love without number. If we desire to perpetuate such bliss, we must perpetuate holiness. The Lord Jesus will not hide His face from us unless we hide our face from Him.

Sin makes the cloud that darkens our Sun: if we will be watchfully obedient and completely consecrated, we may walk in the light, as God is in the light. Here is a sweet promise with a solemn "if". Lord, let me have this "if" in my hand, for as a key it opens this casket.

FOLLOW TO KNOW

*"Let us know, let us pursue
the knowledge of the LORD."*

~ *Hosea 6:3*

Not all at once, but by degrees shall we attain to holy knowledge, little by little. We need not despair, though our progress may be slow, for the Lord will not give us up, however slow of understanding we may be. The Lord delights to make the simple wise.

To know the Triune God, this is life eternal: let us keep to this, for then we shall gain complete instruction. By following on to know the Lord, we learn healing after being torn, and life after death. Experience has its perfect work when the heart follows the trackway of the Lord.

My soul, keep close to Jesus, follow on to know Him, and so you will come to the knowledge of Christ, which is the most excellent of all the sciences. The Holy Ghost will lead you into all truth. Is not this His gracious office? Rely upon Him to fulfill it.

OUT OF SPIRITUAL DEATH

"Then you shall know that I am the LORD,
when I have opened your graves, O My people,
and brought you up from your graves."

~ Ezekiel 37:13

This is the greatest and most remarkable of all changes – to be brought out of the grave of spiritual death, and made to rejoice in the light and liberty of spiritual life. None could work this but the living God.

How well do I remember when I was in the valley full of dry bones! Blessed was the day when sovereign grace sent a man of God to prophesy upon me! Glory be to God for the stirring which that word of faith caused among the dry bones. More blessed still was that heavenly breath from the four winds that made me live!

My new life, even in its pinings and sorrowings, is clear proof to me that the Lord can kill and make alive. He is the only God, and my quickened soul adores Him as the great I AM. As long as I live I will praise Him.

VICTORY WITHOUT BATTLE

"Yet I will have mercy on the house of Judah,
will save them by the LORD their God,
and will not save them by bow, nor by
sword or battle, by horses or horsemen."

~ *Hosea 1:7*

Jehovah Himself will deliver His people, but He will not do it by the ordinary means. Men are slow to render to God the glory due unto His name. If they go to battle with sword and bow, and win, they magnify their own right arm and glory in their horses and horsemen.

For this reason our Jehovah often determines to save His people without second means, that all the honor may be to Himself alone.

Look to the Lord alone, and not to man. Expect to see God all the more clearly when there is no one else to look to. If I have no one at my back, let me be confident if I can feel that the Lord is on my side. Why do I ask for horses and horsemen if Jehovah Himself lifts up His arm for my defense? Let me trust and not be afraid from this day forth.

WITH ME WHEREVER I AM

The LORD is with you.

~ *2 Chronicles 20:17*

If the Lord be with me, it matters little who may desert me. If the Lord be with me, I shall conquer in the battle of life. How can I be sure that the Lord is with me?

For certain He is with me if I am with Him. If I trust in His faithfulness, believe His words, and obey His commands, He is assuredly with me. If I live to honor God, I may be sure that He will honor me.

If I have placed my soul in the hands of God's only-begotten Son, then I may be sure that the Father will put forth all His power to preserve me, that His Son may not be dishonored.

Lord, fulfill this word to me! Be with me in the house, in the street, in the field, in the shop, in the company, and alone. Be with all Your people.

A STRONG HEART

*Wait on the LORD; be of good courage, and He shall
strengthen your heart; wait, I say, on the LORD!*

~ *Psalm 27:14*

Wait! Wait! Let your waiting be on the Lord! He is
worth waiting for. He never disappoints the waiting
soul. While waiting, keep up your spirits. Expect a
great deliverance, and be ready to praise God for it.

"He shall strengthen your heart." This goes at
once to the place where you need help. If the heart
be sound, all the rest of the system will work well.

The heart wants calming and cheering, and both
of these will come if it be strengthened. A forceful
heart rests and rejoices and throbs force into the
whole man.

God is full of strength, and, therefore, He can
impart it to those who need it. Be brave; for the Lord
will impart His strength to you, and you shall be
calm in tempest and glad in sorrow.

Wait on the Lord. I know by long and deep experience that it is good to wait upon the Lord.

THE REACH OF ALMIGHTY GRACE

And it shall come to pass in the place where it was said to them, "You are not My people," there it shall be said to them, "You are sons of the living God."

~ Hosea 1:10

Sovereign grace can make strangers into sons, and the Lord here declares His purpose to deal thus with rebels. Let us join hands and hearts in praising Him.

Some of us were so ungodly that the Lord's Word said to our conscience and heart, "You are not My people." Truly a sad, condemning voice it was.

But now, in the same places from the same ministry and Scripture, we hear a voice saying, "You are the sons of the living God." Does it not give us hope for others? Who is beyond the reach of almighty grace? How can we despair of any, since the Lord has wrought so marvelous a change in us?

He who has kept this one great promise will keep every other; therefore, let us go forward with songs of adoration and confidence.

BROKEN AND SMOKING

A bruised reed He will not break,
and smoking flax He will not quench.

~ Isaiah 42:3

Then I may reckon upon tender treatment from my Lord. Indeed, I feel myself to be at best as weak, as pliant, as worthless as a reed. Alas! I am worse than a reed when it grows by the river, for that at least can hold up its head. I am bruised; sorely, sadly bruised. There is no music in me now. Yet Jesus will not break me; and if He will not, then I mind little what others try to do. Compassionate Lord, I nestle down beneath Your protection and forget my bruises!

Truly I am also fit to be likened to the "smoking flax," whose light is gone, and only its smoke remains. I fear I am rather a nuisance than a benefit. Yet Jesus will not quench me; therefore, I am hopeful.

Lord, kindle me anew and cause me to shine forth to Your glory, and to the extolling of Your tenderness.

FEAR HAS ITS PLACE

Happy is the man that feareth always.

~ Proverbs 28:14 KJV

The fear of the Lord is the beginning and the foundation of all true religion. He is happy who feels a jealous fear of doing wrong. Holy fear looks not only before it leaps, but even before it moves. It is afraid of error, of neglecting duty, of committing sin. It fears ill company, loose talk, and questionable policy. He who foresees evil and escapes it is happier than he who walks carelessly on and is destroyed.

Fear of God is a quiet grace that leads a man along a choice road, of which it is written, "No lion shall be there, nor shall any ravenous beast go up on it" (Isa. 35:9). In both senses he that "feareth always" is made happy.

Solomon had tried both worldliness and holy fear: in the one he found vanity, in the other happiness. Let us not repeat his trial, but abide by his verdict.

COMING IN, GOING OUT

"Blessed shall you be when you come in,
and blessed shall you be when you go out."

~ *Deuteronomy 28:6*

If I keep the commands of my Lord, I may appropriate this promise without question.

This day I will *come into* my house without fear of evil tidings, and I will come into my closet expecting to hear good news from my Lord. I will not be afraid to come in unto myself by self-examination, nor to come into my affairs by a diligent inspection of my business. Oh, for the blessing of the Lord Jesus, who has promised to abide with me.

I must also *go out.* Timidity makes me wish that I could stay within doors and never go into the sinful world. But I must go out in my calling; I must be a defender of the faith and an assailant of evil. Oh, for a blessing upon my going out this day!

Lord, let me go where You lead, on Your errands, under Your command, and in the power of Your Spirit.

SUFFERERS MAKE
STRONG BELIEVERS

*It is good for a man to bear
the yoke in his youth.*

~ Lamentations 3:27

This is as good as a promise. It has been good, it is good, and it will be good for me to bear the yoke.

The yoke of censure is an irksome one, but it prepares a man for future honor. He is not fit to be a leader who has not run the gauntlet of contempt. Praise intoxicates if it be not preceded by abuse. Men who rise to eminence without a struggle usually fall into dishonor.

The yoke of affliction, disappointment, and excessive labor is by no means to be sought for; but when the Lord lays it on us in our youth, it frequently develops a character that glorifies God and blesses the Church.

Come my soul, bow your neck; take up your cross. It was good for you when young; it will not harm you now. For Jesus' sake, shoulder it cheerfully.

WHAT OF MY HOUSE?

*Believe on the Lord Jesus Christ, and you
will be saved, you and your household.*

~ *Acts 16:31*

This verse would suit me if I was dying, and it is all
that I need while I am living. I look away from self,
and I trust the Lord Jesus. I believe in Him; I rest on
Him; I accept Him to be my all.

Lord, I would not run away with half a promise
when You give a whole one. I implore You, save all
my "household." Save the nearest and dearest.

Be gracious to all who dwell under my roof or
work for me. You make this promise to me personally if I believe in the Lord Jesus; I ask You, do as You
have said.

I would go over in my prayer every day the names
of all my brothers and sisters, parents, children,
friends, relatives, and servants and give You no rest
till that word is fulfilled, "and your household."

THE DEW OF HEAVEN

His heavens shall also drop dew.

~ Deuteronomy 33:28

How greatly do I need the dew of the Spirit! Without the Spirit of God I am a dry and withered thing. How sweetly does this dew refresh me! When once favored with it, I feel happy, lively, vigorous, elevated. I want nothing more. The Holy Spirit brings me life and all that life requires. When He bedews me, every means of grace is sweet and profitable.

What a promise is this for me! "His heavens shall also drop dew." I shall be visited with grace. May I, at this very hour, feel the gentle, silent, saturating dew of the Lord! He who has made me to live as the grass lives in the meadow will treat me as He treats the grass; He will refresh me from above. Grass cannot call for dew as I do. Surely the Lord who visits the unpraying plant will answer to His pleading child.

MARK OF DIVINE APPROVAL

Blessed is the man who endures temptation;
for when he has been approved, he will receive
the crown of life which the Lord has
promised to those who love Him.

~ James 1:1

Yes, he is blessed while he is enduring the trial. No eye can see this till he has been anointed with heavenly eye salve. But he must endure it, without rebelling against God, or turning aside from his integrity. He is blessed who has gone through the fire and has not been consumed.

When the test is over, then comes the hallmark of divine approval, "the crown of life." Life is the reward: not mere being, but holy, happy, true existence – the realization of the divine purpose concerning us.

The Lord has promised the crown of life to those who love Him. Only lovers of the Lord will hold out in the hour of trial; the rest will either sink or sulk, or slink back to the world. Do you love the Lord? Truly? Deeply? Wholly? Then that love will be tried, but many waters will not quench it, neither will the floods drown it.

THE SAFEST SHELTER

A man will be as a hiding place from the wind,
and a cover from the tempest.

~ Isaiah 32:2

Who could this Man be but the Son of Man? What a hiding place He has been to His people! He bears the full force of the wind Himself, sheltering those who hide in Him. Why do we stand in the wind when we may so readily and so surely get out of it by hiding behind our Lord? Let us run to Him and be at peace.

Often the wind of trouble rises in its force and becomes a tempest, sweeping everything before it. Things that looked firm, rock in the blast. Our Lord Jesus, the glorious Man, is a cover that is never blown down. In Him we mark the tempest sweeping by, but we ourselves rest in delightful serenity.

Today let us stow ourselves away in our hiding place, and sit and sing under the protection of our Cover. How we love You, Jesus! You are a shelter in the storm.

REWARD IS CERTAIN

*"Whoever gives one of these little ones only
a cup of cold water in the name of a disciple,
assuredly, I say to you, he shall
by no means lose his reward."*

~ Matthew 10:42

I can do that. I can do a kind act toward the Lord's servant. For the sake of the Master, I love the disciples.

How gracious of the Lord to mention so insignificant an action as giving a cup of cold water only! This I can do, however poor; this I may do, however lowly; this I will do, cheerfully.

This, which seems so little, the Lord notices when done to the least of His followers. It is not the cost, the skill, or the quantity that He looks at, but the motive: that which we do to a disciple, because he is a disciple, according to the riches of His grace.

I give a cup of cold water, and He makes me to drink of living water. I give to one of His little ones, and He treats me as one of them. He says, "He shall by no means lose his reward."

LIKE PALM AND CEDAR

The righteous shall flourish like a palm tree,
he shall grow like a cedar in Lebanon.

~ Psalm 92:12

Palms and cedars are "trees of the Lord," and it is by
His care that they flourish. So it is with the saints
of the Lord; they are His own care. These trees are
evergreen and are beautiful in all seasons. Believers
are not sometimes holy and sometimes ungodly; they
stand in the beauty of the Lord under all weathers. The
followers of Jesus are the observed of all observers;
like a city set on a hill, they cannot be hid.

The child of God flourishes like a palm tree,
which pushes all its strength upward. It has no
growth to the right or left, but sends all its force
heavenward and bears its fruit as near the sky as
possible.

The cedar braves all storms and grows near the
eternal snows, the Lord Himself filling it with a sap
that keeps its heart warm and its bough strong.

Lord, so let it be with me.

COMPLETE SAFETY

Of Benjamin he said: "The beloved of the LORD
shall dwell in safety by Him, who shelters him
all the day long; and he shall dwell between His shoulders."
~ *Deuteronomy 33:12*

Yes, there is no safety like that which comes of dwelling near to God. For His best beloved, the Lord can find no surer or safer place. Lord, let me always abide under Your shadow. Nearer and nearer would I come to You, my Lord; and when once especially near You, I would abide there forever.

What a covering the Lord gives to His chosen! Jehovah Himself will cover us. Nothing can come at us when we are thus covered. This covering the Lord will grant us all the day long, however long the day. Lord, let me abide this day consciously beneath this canopy of love, this pavilion of sovereign power.

The Lord is the support and strength of His saints. Lord, let me ever enjoy Your help, and then my arms will be sufficient for me.

THE REASON FOR SINGING

The LORD your God in your midst, the Mighty One,
will save; He will rejoice over you with gladness,
He will quiet you with His love,
He will rejoice over you with singing.

~ Zephaniah 3:17

What a word is this! Jehovah God in the center of His people, in all the majesty of His power! This presence alone suffices to inspire us with peace and hope. We not only have His presence, but He is engaged upon His choice work of salvation. "He will save." Let us not fear any danger for the Lord God is mighty to save.

Nor is this all. He abides evermore the same; He loves, He finds rest in loving, and He will not cease to love. His love gives Him joy. He even finds a theme for song in His beloved. This is exceedingly wonderful. Jehovah Jesus sings a marriage song over His chosen bride. She is to Him His love, His joy, His rest, His song.

O Lord Jesus, by Your immeasurable love to us, teach us to love You, to rejoice in You, and to sing unto You, our Life-psalm.

PERFECT WILLINGNESS

*Your people shall be volunteers
in the day of Your power.*

~ Psalm 110:3

Blessed be the God of grace that it is so! He has a people whom He has chosen from of old to be His peculiar portion. When the day of His power comes and grace displays its omnipotence, they become willing to repent and to believe in Jesus.

None are saved unwillingly, but the will is made sweetly to yield itself. What a wondrous power is this, which never violates the will, and yet rules it!

Now are we willing to be, to do, or to suffer as the Lord wills. If at any time we grow rebellious, He has but to come to us with power, and straightaway we run in the way of His commands with all our hearts. I am willing, I am wholly at Your disposal, Lord; willing and eager to be used for Your holy purposes. O Lord, give me power, as You give me will.

LET TRIALS BLESS

*Knowing that tribulation
worketh patience.*

~ Romans 5:3 KJV

This is a promise in essence; we need patience, and here we see the way of getting it. It is only by enduring that we learn to endure.

You could not learn patience without trouble. Is it not worthwhile to suffer tribulation for the sake of gaining a mind that quietly acquiesces the will of God?

Tribulation in itself works petulance, unbelief, and rebellion. It is only by the sacred alchemy of grace that it is made to work in us patience. We do not thresh the wheat to lay the dust: yet the flail of tribulation does this upon God's floor.

Oh, for grace to let my trials bless me! Why should I wish to halt their gracious operation?

Lord, I ask You to remove my affliction, but I beseech You ten times more to remove my impatience. Precious Jesus, with Your cross engrave the image of Your patience on my heart.

BROAD RIVERS WITHOUT GALLEY

*There the majestic LORD will be for us a place
of broad rivers and streams, in which no galley
with oars will sail, nor majestic ships pass by.*

~ Isaiah 33:21

The Lord will bring to us the greatest good without any of the drawbacks. If a city is favored with broad rivers, it is liable to be attacked by other ships of war. But when the Lord represents the abundance of His bounty, He takes care to shut out fear.

Lord, if You send me wealth, do not let the galley with oars come up in the shape of worldliness or pride. If I have success in holy service, let me never find the galley of self-conceit and self-confidence floating on the waves of my usefulness.

Should I be so supremely happy as to enjoy the light of Your countenance year after year, let me never despise Your feeble saints or allow the vain notion of my own perfection to sail up the broad rivers of my full assurance. Lord, give me that blessing which makes rich without adding sorrow or sin.

DELIVERANCE FROM DUST AND CHAFF

"Surely I will command, and will sift the house of Israel among all nations, as grain is sifted in a sieve; yet not the smallest grain shall fall to the ground."

~ *Amos 9:9*

The sifting process is going on still. Wherever we go, we are still being winnowed and sifted. God's people are being tried "as grain is sifted in a sieve." Sometimes the devil holds the sieve and tosses us up and down with the earnest desire to get rid of us forever. The world lends a willing hand at the same process and shakes us to the right and to the left with great vigor.

Well, let it go on. Thus is the chaff severed from the wheat. Thus is the wheat delivered from dust and chaff. And how great is the mercy that comes to us in the text, "yet not the smallest grain shall fall to the ground." All shall be preserved that is good, true, gracious. Not one of the least of believers shall be lost; neither shall any believer lose anything worth calling a loss.

THE LIFE-GIVING STREAM

*It shall be that every living thing that
moves, wherever the rivers go, will live.*

~ *Ezekiel 47:9*

The living waters in the prophet's vision flowed into
the Dead Sea and carried life with them, even into
that stagnant lake. Where grace goes, spiritual life is
the immediate and everlasting consequence. Grace
proceeds sovereignly according to the will of God,
even as a river in all its windings follows its own
sweet will; and wherever it comes it does not wait
for life to come to it, but it creates life by its own
quickening flow.

Lord, let the living water flow to my family and
my friends, and let it not pass me by. I desire to bathe
in it, to swim in it. I need life more abundantly. Come
to me, till every part of my nature is vividly energetic
and intensely active.

Living God, fill me with Your own life, that, like
Aaron's rod, I may bud and blossom and bring forth
fruit unto Your glory.

THE SACRIFICE
HAS BEEN ACCEPTED

If the LORD had desired to kill us, He would not have accepted a burnt offering and a grain offering from our hands, nor would He have shown us all these things.

~ Judges 13:23

This is a sort of promise deduced by logic. It was not likely that the Lord had revealed to Manoah and his wife that a son would be born to them, and yet had it in His heart to destroy them. Let us, too, follow this line of argument.

The Father has accepted the great sacrifice of Calvary and has declared Himself well pleased. The Lord has shown us our election, our adoption, our union to Christ, our marriage to the Well-beloved: how can He now destroy us?

The promises are loaded with blessings, which necessitate our being preserved unto eternal life. It is not possible for the Lord to cast us away and yet fulfill His covenant. The past assures us, and the future reassures us.

AMONG THE REDEEMED

There! A people dwelling alone,
not reckoning itself among the nations.

~ Numbers 23:9

Who would wish to dwell among the nations and to be numbered with them?

The Lord would have His people follow a separate path as to the world. We are set apart by the divine decree, purchase, and calling, and our inward experience has made us greatly to differ from men of the world. Therefore, our place is not with them, but in the narrow way where all true pilgrims must follow their Lord.

This may not reconcile us to the world's cold shoulder and sneers, but our names are not in the same book; we are not of the same seed; we are not bound for the same place; neither are we trusting to the same guide.

Therefore, it is well that we are not of their number. Only let us be found in the number of the redeemed, and we are content to be odd and solitary to the end of the chapter.

THE DIVINE LIGHT IN DARKNESS

You will light my lamp.

~ *Psalm 18:28*

It may be that my soul sits in darkness; if this be of a spiritual kind, no human power can bring me light. But God can enlighten my darkness, and at once light my candle. Even though I may be surrounded by a darkness that can be felt, He can break the gloom and make it bright around me.

The mercy is that if He lights the candle, none can blow it out; neither will it go out for lack of substance nor burn out of itself after many hours. The lights that the Lord kindled in the beginning are shining still.

Let me then, like the nightingale, sing in the dark. Expectation shall furnish me with music, and hope shall pitch the tune. Whatever has made my darkness now; God will bring the light. My eyes are unto Him alone. I shall soon have the candles of the Lord shining about me. Hallelujah!

WORK IS DONE; REST IN HIM

*There remains therefore a rest
for the people of God.*

~ Hebrews 4:9

God has provided a Sabbath, and it remains for the people of God to enter into it.

Come, then, let us labor to enter into this rest. Let us cease from our own works, as God did from His. Let us find solace in the finished work of our Lord Jesus. Everything is fully done: justice demands no more. Great peace is our portion in Christ Jesus.

As to the work of grace in the soul, and the work of the Lord in the souls of others, let us cast these burdens upon the Lord and rest in Him. When the Lord gives us a yoke to bear, He does so that by taking it up we may find rest.

By faith we labor to enter into the rest of God, and we renounce all rest in self-satisfaction or indolence. Jesus Himself is perfect rest, and we are filled to the brim in Him.

TO GLORIFY CHRIST JESUS

*"He will glorify Me, for He will take
of what is Mine and declare it to you."*

~ John 16:14

The Holy Ghost Himself cannot better glorify the Lord than by showing to us Christ's own things. Jesus is His own best commendation. There is no adorning Him except with His own gold.

The Comforter shows us that which He has received of our Lord Jesus. He has a way of opening our minds and of opening the Scriptures, and by this double process He sets forth our Lord to us. He shows us the things themselves and this is a great privilege.

Let us seek the illumination of the Spirit, not to gratify our curiosity, or to bring personal comfort, but to glorify the Lord Jesus. Oh, to have worthy ideas of Him; to have such vivid impressions of His person, work, and glory that we may with heart and soul cry out His praise!

Where there is a heart enriched by the Holy Ghost's teaching, there will be a Savior glorified beyond expression.

OPEN YOUR MOUTH

*"Open your mouth wide,
and I will fill it."*

~ *Psalm 81:10*

What an encouragement to pray! The Lord would have us request great blessings! When a man is earnest, he opens his mouth wide, and our text urges us to be fervent in our supplications.

Yet it also means that we may be bold with God and ask large blessings at His hands. Read the whole verse, "I am the LORD your God, who brought you out of the land of Egypt; open your mouth wide, and I will fill it." Because the Lord has given us so much, He invites us to ask for more.

See how the little birds in their nests seem to be all mouth when the mother comes to feed them. Let it be the same with us. God is ready to fill us if we are only ready to be filled.

The opened mouth shall be filled by the Lord Himself. So be it unto us, Lord, today.

October

A Covenant He Remembers

He has given food to those who fear Him;
He will ever be mindful of His covenant.

~ Psalm 111:5

Those who fear God need not fear or want. Through all these long years the Lord has always found meat for His children, whether they have been in the wilderness or by the brook Cherith. So we doubt not that He will continue to feed us till we want no more.

As to the higher and greater blessings of the covenant of grace, He will never cease to supply them as our case demands. He is mindful that He made the covenant, and He is mindful to love us, keep us, and comfort us.

Even when we are unmindful of God, He is graciously mindful of us. He cannot forget His Son who is the Surety of the Covenant, or His Holy Spirit who actively carries out the covenant, or His own honor, which is bound up with the covenant.

Hence the foundation of God stands sure, and no believer shall lose his divine inheritance.

COMFORT EN ROUTE HOME

And Joseph said to his brethren, "I am dying;
but God will surely visit you, and bring you out
of this land to the land of which He swore
to Abraham, to Isaac, and to Jacob."

~ Genesis 50:24

Egypt was never the same to Israel after Joseph was dead, nor can the world again be to some of us what it was when our beloved ones were alive.

But see how the pain of that sad death was alleviated! They had a promise that the living God would visit them. A visit from Jehovah! What a consolation! Lord, visit us this day; though indeed we are not worthy that You should come under our roof.

But more was promised: the Lord would bring them out. They would find in Egypt a cold welcome when Joseph was dead, but it was not to be so forever; they would come out of it by a divine deliverance and march to the land of promise.

We shall not weep here forever. We shall be called home to the Glory Land to join our dear ones.

REFLECTORS OF
THE LORD'S BEAUTY

As for me, I will see Your face in righteousness;
I shall be satisfied when I awake in Your likeness.

~ *Psalm 17:15*

Men of the world have their treasure in this world, but men of the world to come look higher and further.

Our possession is twofold. We have God's *presence* here and His *likeness* hereafter. Here we behold the face of the Lord in righteousness, for we are justified in Christ Jesus. The glory of God in the face of Jesus yields us heaven below, and it will be to us the heaven of heaven above.

But seeing does not end it: we are to be changed into that which we gaze upon. We shall sleep a while and then wake up to find ourselves as mirrors that reflect the beauties of our Lord.

Faith sees God with a transforming look. The heart receives the image of Jesus into its own depths till the character of Jesus is imprinted on the soul. To see God and to be like Him – what more can I desire?

THE MIGHTY MAGNET

"And I, if I am lifted up from the earth,
will draw all peoples to Myself."

~ *John 12:32*

Come, be encouraged. You fear that you cannot draw a congregation. Try the preaching of a crucified and risen Savior, for this is the greatest "draw" ever yet manifested among men. What drew you to Christ but Christ? What draws you to Him now but His own blessed self? Jesus has held you and will hold you even to the end. Why, then, doubt His power to draw others?

No sort of man is beyond His drawing power. Old and young, rich and poor, ignorant and learned, all men shall feel the attractive force. Jesus is the one magnet. Let us not think of any other. Jesus Himself must draw men to Himself, and Jesus is quite equal to the work in every case.

As workers for the Lord, work in His own way and draw with the Lord's own cords. Draw to Christ, and draw by Christ, for then Christ will draw by you.

AT GOD'S BIDDING

Then the remnant of Jacob shall be in the midst
of many peoples, like dew from the Lord,
like showers on the grass, that tarry
for no man nor wait for the sons of men.

~ *Micah 5:7*

If this be true of the literal Israel, much more is it true of the spiritual Israel, the believing people of God. When saints are what they should be, they are an incalculable blessing to those among whom they are scattered.

They are as the dew; for in a quiet, unobtrusive manner they refresh those around them. Silently but effactually they minister to the life, growth, and joy of those who dwell with them. Little as individuals, they are, when united, all sufficient for the purposes of love that the Lord fulfills through them. Lord, make us like the dew!

Godly people are as showers that come at God's bidding without man's leave and license. They work for God whether men desire it or not; they no more ask human permission than the rain does. Lord, make us thus boldly prompt and free in Your service, wherever our lot is cast.

THE LEADERSHIP OF OUR GUIDE

*"However, when He, the Spirit of truth,
has come, He will guide you into all truth."*

~ John 16:13

Truth is like a vast cavern that we desire to enter, but we are not able to traverse alone. At the entrance it is clear and bright; but if we would go further and explore its innermost recesses, we must have a guide or we shall lose ourselves.

The Holy Spirit, who knows all truth, is the appointed guide of all true believers, and He conducts them from one inner chamber to another, so that they behold the deep things of God, and His secret is made plain to them.

What a promise! "All truth" we wish to learn, that we may not be one-sided and out of balance. We would not be willingly ignorant of any part of revelation, lest we should miss blessing or incur sin.

The Spirit of God has come that He may guide us into all truth: let us with obedient hearts hear His words and follow His lead.

ALWAYS FIRST IN FELLOWSHIP

*Go, tell His disciples – and Peter – that He is
going before you into Galilee; there you
will see Him, as He said to you.*

~ Mark 16:7

Where He appointed to meet His disciples, there He would be. Jesus keeps His tryst. If He promises to meet us at the mercy seat, or in public worship, we may depend upon it that He will be there. We may stay away from the appointed meeting place, but He never does, "Where two or three are gathered together in My name, I am there" (Matt. 18:20).

Jesus is always first in fellowship: His heart is with His people, His delight is in them, He is never slow to meet with them. In all fellowship He goes before us.

He reveals Himself to those who come after Him, "There you will see Him." To see Him is to be filled with joy and peace. And we shall see Him, for He promises to come to those who believe in Him and He does everything according to His word of promise, "As He said to you."

NEVER ALONE

*You shall no longer
be termed Forsaken.*

~ Isaiah 62:4

An abyss of misery yawns in that word Forsaken. Forsaken by one who pledged his honor! Forsaken by a friend so long tried and trusted! Forsaken by a dear relative! Forsaken by all! This is woe indeed, yet it may be patiently borne if the Lord will take us up.

What must it be to feel forsaken of God? Think of that bitterest of cries, "My God, My God, why have You forsaken Me?" (Matt. 27:46). Have we ever in any degree tasted the gall of Forsaken in that sense? If so, let us beseech our Lord to save us from any repetition of so unspeakable a sorrow. May such darkness never return!

The reverse of all this is that superlative word, *Hephzibah*, "the Lord delights in you." This turns weeping into dancing. Let those who dreamed that they were forsaken hear the Lord say, "I will never leave you nor forsake you."

WHAT SANCTIFIES OUR OFFERINGS?

*The priest shall put some of the blood on
the horns of the altar of sweet incense before the LORD.*

~ Leviticus 4:7

The altar of incense is where saints present their prayers and praises, and it is delightful to think it is sprinkled with the blood of the Great Sacrifice. This is what makes our worship acceptable with Jehovah: He sees the blood of His Son, and therefore accepts our homage.

Sin mingles even with our holy things; and our best repentance, faith, prayer, and thanksgiving could not be received of God were it not for the atoning sacrifice. "The blood" is the foundation of comfort and hope. It gives strength to prayer. It is "before the Lord," and therefore it ought to be before us. It is there to sanctify our offerings and gifts.

So let us pray with confidence, since the Victim is offered, the merit has been pleaded, the blood is within the veil, and the prayers of believers must be sweet unto the Lord.

OPEN DOOR OF COMMUNION

*"I have set before you an open door,
and no one can shut it."*

~ Revelation 3:8

Saints who remain faithful to the truth of God, and live and die by the Word, have an open door before them.

I will enter in by the open door of communion with God. Who shall say no? Jesus has removed my sin and given me His righteousness, therefore I may freely enter.

I have also before me an open door into the mysteries of the Word. I may enter into the deep things of God. No promise and no doctrine are locked up against me.

An open door of access is before me in private, and an open door of usefulness in public. God will hear me; God will use me. Some may try to shut me up or shut me out, but all in vain.

Soon shall I see an open door into heaven: then I shall go in unto my Lord and King, and be with God eternally shut in.

FREE TO TRAVEL

*"I will strengthen them in the LORD, and they shall
walk up and down in His name," says the LORD.*

~ *Zechariah 10:12*

This is a solace for sick saints who have grown faint
and fear that they shall never rise from the bed of
doubt and fear. But the great Physician can both
remove the disease and take away the weakness that
has come of it. Our strength is far better in God than
in self. In ourselves it would be sadly limited, but in
God it knows no bounds.

When strength is given, the believer uses it.
He walks up and down in the name of the Lord.
What an enjoyment it is to walk after illness, and
what a delight to be strong in the Lord after a
season of weakness! We are free to travel at our ease
throughout Immanuel's land.

Come, my heart, be no more sick and sorry;
Jesus bids you be strong and walk with God in holy
contemplation. Obey His word of love.

MARK OF COVENANT GRACE

*The LORD your God will circumcise your heart
and the heart of your descendants, to love
the LORD your God with all your heart and
with all your soul, that you may live.*

~ Deuteronomy 30:6

Note the words, "The Lord your God." He alone can deal effectually with our hearts and take away their carnality. To make us love God with all our hearts and souls is a miracle of grace that only He can work. We must look to the Lord alone for this and never be satisfied with anything short of it.

Note where this circumcision is wrought: it is not of the flesh, but of the spirit. It is the essential mark of the covenant of grace. We must see to it that we trust in no outward ritual, but are sealed in heart by the operation of the Holy Ghost.

Note what the result is, "that you may live." To be carnally minded is death. In the overcoming of the flesh we find life and peace. Oh, that God may complete His gracious work upon us, that we may live unto Him.

A TRIPLE PROMISE

"If My people who are called by My name will humble themselves, and pray and seek My face, and turn from their wicked ways, then I will hear from heaven, and will forgive their sin and heal their land."

~ 2 Chronicles 7:14

Called by the name of the Lord, we are nevertheless sinful men. What a mercy it is that our God is ready to forgive! Whenever we sin let us hasten to the mercy seat of our God, seeking pardon.

We are to humble ourselves. Should we not be humbled by the fact that after receiving so much love, we still sin? Lord, we bow before You and own our grievous ingratitude.

We are to pray for mercy, cleansing, and deliverance from the power of sin. Lord, hear us even now, and shut not out our cry. In this prayer we are to seek the Lord's face. With this must go our own turning from evil, God cannot turn to us unless we turn from sin.

Then comes the triple promise of hearing, pardon, and healing. Father, we pray You grant us these at once.

NEVER ASHAMED

*"Therefore whoever confesses Me before men,
him I will also confess before My Father who is in heaven."*

~ Matthew 10:32

It is a great joy to me to confess my Lord. Whatever my faults may be, I am not ashamed of my Jesus.

Sweet is the prospect that the text sets before me! Friends forsake and enemies exult, but the Lord does not disown His servant. My Lord will own me even here and give me new tokens of His favorable regard. But there comes a day when I must stand before the Father. What bliss to think that Jesus will confess me then! He will say, "This man truly trusted Me, and was willing to be reproached for My name's sake; and therefore I acknowledge him as Mine."

It will be an honor beyond all honors for the Lord Jesus to confess us in the presence of the divine Majesty in the heavens. Never let me be ashamed to own my Lord. Shall I blush to own Him who promises to own me?

SUSTAINED BY FEEDING

*"As the living Father sent Me, and I live
because of the Father, so he who feeds
on Me will live because of Me."*

~ John 6:57

We live by virtue of our union with the Son of God. As God-man Mediator, the Lord Jesus lives by the self-existent Father who has sent Him; and in the same manner, we live by the Savior who has quickened us. He who is the source of our life is also the sustenance of it. On Jesus Himself we feed.

This is set forth to us in the Lord's Supper, but it is actually enjoyed by us when we meditate upon our Lord, believe in Him with appropriating faith, take Him into ourselves by love, and assimilate Him by the power of the inner life. We are entreated to eat abundantly, and it will be to our infinite profit to do so when Jesus is our meat and our drink.

Lord, thank You that what is a necessity of my new life is also its greatest delight. At this hour I feed on You.

ONE WITH CHRIST

"Because I live, you will live also."

~ John 14:19

Jesus has made the life of believers in Him as certain as His own. As sure as the Head lives, the members live also. His death has put away our transgressions and loosed the bonds that held us under the death sentence.

Jesus has made the life of His people as eternal as His own. How can they die as long as He lives, seeing they are one with Him? When, under great temptation, you fear that you will one day fall by the hand of the enemy, let this reassure you. You will never lose your spiritual life, for it is hid with Christ in God.

You do not doubt the immortality of the Lord; therefore, do not think that He will let you die, since you are one with Him. The argument for your life is His life, and of that you can have no fear. Therefore, rest in the living Lord.

HOLY FEAR

He who fears the commandment
will be rewarded.

~ Proverbs 13:13

Holy awe of God's Word is at a great discount. We accept the inspired Book as infallible and prove our esteem by our obedience. We have no terror of the Word, but we have a filial awe of it. We are not in fear of its penalties, because we have a fear of its commands.

This holy fear of the commandment produces the restfulness of humility, which is far sweeter than the recklessness of pride. It becomes a guide to us in our movements, a drag when we are going downhill, and a stimulus when we are climbing it.

The ungodly may ridicule our deep reverence for the Word of the Lord, but what of that? The prize of our high calling is a sufficient consolation for us. The rewards of obedience make us scorn the scorning of the scorner.

TEARS, THEN JOYFUL HARVEST

*Those who sow in tears
shall reap in joy.*

~ Psalm 126:5

Weeping times are suitable for sowing: we do not want the ground to be too dry. The salt of prayerful tears will give the good seed a flavor, which will preserve it from the worm. Instead of stopping our sowing because of our weeping, let us redouble our efforts because the season is so propitious.

Our heavenly seed could not fitly be sown laughing. Deep sorrow and concern for the souls of others are a far more fit accompaniment of godly teaching than levity.

Come, then, my heart, sow on in your weeping, for you have the promise of a joyful harvest. You shall reap and see results of your labor. It shall come to you in so large a measure as to give you joy.

When your eyes are dim with silver tears, think of the golden corn. Bear cheerfully the present toil and disappointment; for the harvest day will fully recompense you.

REGULATED CHASTISEMENT

"I will correct thee in measure."

~ Jeremiah 30:11 KJV

To be left uncorrected would be a fatal sign. As many as God tenderly loves, He rebukes and chastens: those for whom He has no esteem He allows to fatten themselves without fear, like bullocks for the slaughter. It is in love that our heavenly Father uses the rod upon His children.

Yet see, the correction is "in measure": He gives us love without measure, but chastisement "in measure." It is the measure of wisdom, the measure of sympathy, the measure of love, by which our chastisement is regulated. Far be it from us to rebel against appointments so divine.

Lord, if You stand by to measure the bitter drops into my cup, it is for me cheerfully to take that cup and drink according to Your directions, saying, "May Your will be done."

FROM EVERY SIN

He will save His people from their sins.

~ Matthew 1:21

Lord, save me from my sins. Save me from past sins, that the habit of them may not hold me captive. Save me from constitutional sins, that I may not be the slave of my own weaknesses. Save me from the sins that are continually under my eye, that I may not lose my horror of them. Save me from secret sins, sins unperceived by me. Save me from sudden and surprising sins: let me not be carried off by a rush of temptation. Let not any iniquity have dominion over me.

You alone can do this. You know temptation, for You were tempted. You know sin, for You bore the weight of it. You can save me from sinning and save me when I have sinned.

It is promised in Your very name that You will do this. Save me unto holiness of life, that the name of Jesus may be glorified in me.

GOD'S MULTIPLICATION TABLE

"A little one shall become a thousand, and a small one a strong nation. I, the LORD, will hasten it in its time."

~ Isaiah 60:22

Works for the Lord often begin on a small scale, and they are none the worse for this. Feebleness educates faith, brings God near, and wins glory for His name. A mustard seed is the smallest among seeds, and yet it becomes a tree-like plant with branches, which lodge the birds of heaven.

We may begin with one, and that "a little one," and yet it will "become a thousand." The Lord is great at the multiplication table. How often did he say to His lone servant, "I will multiply you!" Trust in the Lord.

"A small one." Only one star shines out at first in the evening, but soon the sky is crowded with countless lights.

"I, the LORD, will hasten it." It will be done all in due time. When the Lord hastens, His speed is glorious.

PLEAD HIS OWN PROMISE

*"Therefore, You, O Lord God, have spoken it,
and with Your blessing let the house
of Your servant be blessed forever."*

~ 2 Samuel 7:29

Anything that the Lord God has spoken we should receive as true and plead it at the throne.

How sweet to quote what our own God has spoken! How precious to use a "therefore," which the promise suggests, as David does in this verse!

We pray not because we doubt, but because we believe. No, Lord, we cannot doubt You: we are persuaded that every word of Yours is a sure foundation for the boldest expectation. We say to You, "Do as You have said." Bless Your servant's house. Heal our sick; restore those who wander; give us food and raiment according to Your word. Prosper our undertakings; especially succeed our endeavors to make known Your gospel. Let the blessing flow on to future generations; and as long as any of our race remains on earth, may they remain true to You. O Lord, "let the house of Your servant be blessed."

HARVEST OF LIGHT
AND GLADNESS

Light is sown for the righteous,
and gladness for the upright in heart.

~ Psalm 97:11

Righteousness is often costly to the man who keeps to it at all hazards, but in the end it will return an infinite profit. A holy life is like sowing seed: much is going out, and is seemingly buried in the soil, never to be gathered up again. Yet "light is sown," it lies latent: none can see it, but it is sown. It must manifest itself one day.

The Lord has set a harvest for the sowers of light, and they shall reap it. Then shall come their gladness; sheaves of joy for seeds of light. Their heart was upright before the Lord, though men gave them no credit for it. They had to wait: but the light was sown for them, and gladness was being prepared on their behalf by the Lord of the harvest.

Take courage! We need not be in a hurry; soon shall our souls possess light and gladness.

GODLY STABILITY

*"I will make you to this people a fortified bronze wall;
and they will fight against you, but they shall not
prevail against you; for I am with you to
save you and deliver you," says the LORD.*

~ Jeremiah 15:20

Stability in the fear and faith of God will make a man like a wall of brass, which no one can batter down or break.

Against uncompromising men of truth this age of shams will fight tooth and nail. Nothing seems to offend Satan and his seed like decision. They attack holy firmness even as the Assyrians besieged fenced cities. The joy is that they cannot prevail against those whom God has made strong in His strength. Carried about with every wind of doctrine, others only need to be blown upon and away they go; but those who love the doctrines of grace stand like rocks in the midst of raging seas.

Jehovah will save and deliver faithful souls from all the assaults of the adversary. We dare not budge an inch, for the Lord Himself holds us in our place, and there we will abide forever.

GOD FIRST; THEN EXTRAS

*"Seek first the kingdom of God and His righteousness,
and all these things shall be added to you."*

~ *Matthew 6:33*

Let your life open in the same way. Seek with your whole soul, first and foremost, the kingdom of God as the place of your citizenship, and His righteousness as the character of your life. As for the rest, it will come from the Lord Himself without your being anxious concerning it. All that is needful for this life and godliness "shall be added to you."

What a promise this is! Food, raiment, home, and so forth, God undertakes to add to you while you seek Him. You mind His business, and He will mind ours. And just so, all that we need of earthly things we shall have thrown in with the kingdom.

Away with anxious care; set all your mind upon seeking the Lord. Trust in God is an estate, and likeness to God is a heavenly inheritance.

BECAUSE OF US

*"For the elect's sake those days
will be shortened."*

~ Matthew 24:22

For the sake of His elect, the Lord withholds many judgments and shortens others. In great tribulations the fire would devour all were it not that, out of regard to His elect, the Lord damps the flame.

What an honor is thus put upon saints! How diligently they ought to use their influence with their Lord! He will hear their prayers for sinners, and bless their efforts for their salvation. Many a sinner lives because of the prayers of a mother, or wife, or daughter, to whom the Lord has respect.

Have we used aright the singular power with which the Lord entrusts us? Do we pray for our country, for other lands, and for the age? Do we, in times of war, famine, pestilence, stand out as intercessors, pleading that the days may be shortened? Let us get to our knees and never rest till Christ appears.

HIS SERVICE, FACE, NAME

*His servants shall serve Him. They shall see
His face, and His name shall be on their foreheads.*

~ Revelation 22:3-4

Three choice blessings will be ours in the Glory Land.

"*His servants shall serve Him.*" No other lords shall oppress us. We shall serve Jesus always, perfectly, without weariness. This is heaven to a saint: in all things to serve Christ and to be owned by Him as His servant is our soul's high ambition for eternity.

"*They shall see His face.*" This makes the service delightful: indeed, it is the present reward of service. To see the face of Jesus is the utmost favor that the most faithful servant of the Lord can ask. What more could Moses ask than "Let me see Your face"?

"*His name shall be on their foreheads.*" They gaze upon their Lord till His name is photographed upon their brows. He acknowledges them, and they acknowledge Him.

O Lord, give us these three things in their beginnings now, that we may possess them in their fullness!

SINS OF IGNORANCE

*It shall be forgiven them,
for it was unintentional.*

~ *Numbers 15:25*

Because of ignorance, we may not be fully aware of our sins. We may be, as a service to God, that which He has never commanded and can never accept.

The Lord knows every unintentional sin of ignorance. This may alarm us, yet faith spies comfort, for the Lord will see to it that stains unseen by us shall yet be washed away.

Jesus, the true Priest, has made atonement for all the congregation of the children of Israel. His precious blood cleanses us from all sin. Whether our eyes have seen it and wept over it or not, God has seen it, Christ has atoned for it, the Spirit bears witness to the pardon of it, and so we have a three-fold peace.

Father, I praise Your divine knowledge, which perceives my iniquities, provides atonement, and delivers me from the guilt of them, even before I know that I am guilty.

MAINTAIN THE DIFFERENCE

*"I will make a difference between My people and
your people. Tomorrow this sign shall be."*

~ *Exodus 8:23*

Pharaoh has a people, and the Lord has a people.
These may dwell together, and seem to fare alike,
but there is a division between them, and the Lord
will make it apparent. There shall be great difference
between the men of the world and the people of
Jehovah's choice.

It is very conspicuous in the conversion of believers when their sin is put away, while unbelievers
remain under condemnation. From that moment
believers become a distinct race, come under a new
discipline, and enjoy new blessings. Their homes,
henceforth, are free from the grievous swarms of
evils, which defile and torment many families.

Rest assured that though you have your troubles,
you are saved from swarms of worse ones that infest
the homes and hearts of the servants of the world's
prince. The Lord has put a division; see to it that
you keep up the division in spirit, aim, character,
and company.

THROUGH CLEANSING

*"I will sprinkle clean water on you,
and you shall be clean; I will cleanse you from
all your filthiness and from all your idols."*

~ Ezekiel 36:25

What an exceeding joy is this! He who has purified us with the blood of Jesus will also cleanse us by the water of the Holy Spirit. God has said it, and so it must be, "You shall be clean." Lord, we feel and mourn our uncleanness, and it is cheering to be assured by Your own mouth that we shall be clean.

He will deliver us from our worst sins; these shall be so purged always as never to return. He will also cleanse us from all our idols; that which we have idolized shall either be broken from us, or we shall be broken off from it.

It is God who speaks of what He Himself will do. Therefore is this word established and sure, and we may boldly look for that which it guarantees us.

IMMORTAL UNTIL THE LORD'S WORK IS DONE

*I shall not die, but live,
and declare the works of the LORD.*

~ *Psalm 118:17*

Is my case like that of David? Are there multitudes against me, and few on my side? Does unbelief bid me lie down and die in despair – a defeated man? Do my enemies begin to dig my grave?

What then? Shall I yield to the whisper of fear and give up the battle, and with it give up all hope? Far from it. There is life in me yet, "I shall not die." Vigor will return and remove my weakness, "I shall live." The Lord lives, and I shall live also.

I shall speak of the present trouble as another instance of the wonder-working faithfulness and love of my God. Those who would gladly measure me for my coffin had better wait a bit, for "the LORD has chastened me severely, but He has not given me over to death" (Ps. 118:18). Till the Lord wills it, no vault can close upon me.

November

PERFECTION AND PRESERVATION

He who calls you is faithful,
who also will do it.

~ 1 Thessalonians 5:24

What will He do? He will sanctify us wholly. He will carry on the work of purification till we are perfect in every part. He will preserve our "whole spirit, soul, and body" blameless until His coming. He will not allow us to fall from grace, nor come under the dominion of sin.

Who will do this? The Lord has called us out of darkness into His marvelous light, out of death in sin into eternal life in Christ Jesus. Only He can do this.

Why will He do it? Because He is "faithful" – faithful to His own promise, which is pledged to save the believer; faithful to His Son, whose reward it is that His people shall be presented to Him faultless; faithful to the work which He has commenced in us.

Come, my soul, here is a grand feast. There may be fogs without, but there should be sunshine within.

HEAVENLY WEALTH

*No good thing will He withhold
from those who walk uprightly.*

~ Psalm 84:11

Many pleasing things the Lord may withhold, but "no good thing." He is the best judge of what is good for us.

Holiness is a good thing, and this He will work in us freely. Victory over evil tendencies and evil habits, He will gladly grant.

Full assurance He will bestow, near communion with Himself, access into all truth, and boldness with prevalence at the mercy seat. If we have not these, it is from want of faith to receive, and not from any unwillingness of God to give. A calm, heavenly frame, great patience, and fervent love – all these will He give to holy diligence. But note that we must "walk uprightly." If we walk foully, God cannot give us favors, for that would be a premium upon sin.

The way of uprightness is the way of heavenly wealth – wealth so large as to include every good thing.

IN GOD'S TIME

*"The vision is yet for an appointed time; but at the end
it will speak, and it will not lie. Though it tarries,
wait for it; because it will surely come, it will not tarry."*

~ Habakkuk 2:3

Mercy may seem slow but it is sure. The Lord, in unfailing wisdom, has appointed a time for outgoings of His gracious power, and God's time is the best time. We are in a hurry; the vision of blessing excites our desire and hastens longings; but the Lord will keep His appointment. He never is before or behind His time.

God's Word is a living Word, from the living God; and though it may seem to linger, God's train is never behind time. It is only a matter of patience, and shall soon see for ourselves the faithfulness of the Lord. No promise of His shall fail; "it will not lie." No promise of His will be lost in silence, "it will speak." No promise of His shall need to be renewed, "it will not tarry."

My soul, can you not wait for your God? Rest in Him, and be still in unutterable peacefulness.

YOU MAKE THE TRENCHES

*"Thus says the LORD: 'Make this valley full of ditches.'
For thus says the LORD: 'You shall not see wind,
nor shall you see rain; yet that valley shall
be filled with water, so that you, your cattle,
and your animals may drink.'"*

~ 2 Kings 3:16-17

Three armies were perishing of thirst, and the Lord interposed. Although He sent neither cloud nor rain, He supplied an abundance of water. God is not dependent upon ordinary methods, but can surprise His people with novelties of wisdom and power. Thus are we made to see more of God than ordinary processes could have revealed.

Have we this day grace enough to make ditches into which the divine blessing may flow? Sadly, we too often fail in the exhibition of true and practical faith. Let us this day be on the outlook for answers to prayer. As the child who went to a meeting to pray for rain took an umbrella with her, so let us truly and practically expect the Lord to bless us.

Let us make the valley full of ditches and expect to see them all filled.

WHAT IS PAINFUL WILL END

"I will not contend forever, nor will I always be angry;
for the spirit would fail before Me,
and the souls which I have made."

~ Isaiah 57:16

Our heavenly Father seeks our instruction, not our destruction. His contention *with* us has a kind intention *toward* us. We think the Lord is long in His chastisements, but that is because we are short in our patience. The night may drag its weary length along, but it must in the end give place to cheerful day. The Lord loves His chosen too well to be always angry with them.

Courage, dear heart! The Lord will soon end His chiding. He who made you knows how frail you are and how little you can bear. He will handle tenderly that which He has fashioned so delicately.

Therefore, be not afraid because of the painful present, for it hastens to a happy future. His little wrath shall be followed by great mercies.

DELIGHT AND DESIRES

Delight yourself also in the LORD,
and He shall give you the desires of your heart.

~ Psalm 37:4

Delight in God has a transforming power and lifts a man above the gross desires of our fallen nature. Delight in Jehovah is not only sweet in itself, but it sweetens the whole soul, till the longings of the heart become such that the Lord can safely promise to fulfill them.

If we will let our heart be filled with God till it runs over with delight, then the Lord Himself will take care that we shall not want for any good thing. Instead of going abroad for joys, let us stay at home with God and drink waters out of our own fountain

For a while we may have disappointments; but if these bring us nearer to the Lord, they are things to be prized exceedingly, for they will in the end secure to us the fulfillment of all our right desires.

TRUE HUMILITY REWARDED

"He who humbles himself will be exalted."

~ Luke 18:14

It ought not to be difficult for us to humble ourselves – what have we to be proud of? If we are sensible and honest we shall be little in our own eyes. Our one and only appeal must be to mercy, "God be merciful to me."

Here is a cheering word from the throne. We shall be exalted by the Lord if we humble ourselves. For us the way upward is downhill. When we are stripped of self, we are clothed with humility, which is the best of wear.

The Lord will exalt us in peace and happiness of mind; in knowledge of His Word and fellowship with Himself; and in the enjoyment of sure pardon and justification.

The Lord puts His honors upon those who can wear them to the honor of the Giver. Both God and good men unite to honor modest worth.

Lord, sink me in self that I may rise in You.

THE MAGNITUDE OF GRACE

*"My grace is sufficient for you, for My strength
is made perfect in weakness."*

~ *2 Corinthians 12:9*

This is a precious word from our Lord! God's grace is enough for me! I should think so. Is not the sky enough for the bird, and the ocean enough for the fish? He who is sufficient for earth and heaven is certainly able to meet the case of one poor worm like me.

Let us then fall back upon our God and His grace. If He does not remove our grief He will enable us to bear it. His strength shall be poured into us till a nothing shall be victor over all the high and mighty ones.

It is better for us to have God's strength than our own; for if we were a thousand times as strong as we are, it would amount to nothing in the face of the enemy; and if we could be weaker than we are, which is scarcely possible, yet we could do all things through Christ.

NECESSARY KNOWLEDGE

*"Thus they shall know that I, the LORD their God,
am with them, and they, the house of Israel,
are My people," says the Lord GOD.*

~ *Ezekiel 34:30*

It is one thing to *hope* that God is with us and another thing to *know* that He is so. Faith saves us, but assurance satisfies us. We take God to be our God when we believe in Him, but we get the joy of Him when we know that He is ours and we are His.

It is when we enjoy covenant blessings and see our Lord Jesus raised up for us that we come to a clear knowledge of favor of God toward us. Not by law, but by grace, we learn that we are the Lord's people. Let us look to the Lord alone. As we see Jesus shall we see our salvation.

Lord, send us such a floodtide of Your love that we shall be washed beyond the mire of doubt and fear.

WALK WITHOUT STUMBLING

He will not allow your foot to be moved.

~ *Psalm 121:3*

If the Lord will not allow it, neither men nor devils can do it. How greatly would they rejoice if they could give us a disgraceful fall, drive us from our position, and bury us out of memory! They could do this to their heart's content were it not for one hindrance, and only one: the Lord will not allow it; and if *He* does not allow it, *we* shall not allow it.

When traveling along mountain paths one is constantly exposed to the slipping of the foot. Where the way is high, the head is apt to swim and then the feet soon slide. He, who throughout life is enabled to keep himself upright and to walk without stumbling, has the best of reasons for gratitude. What with pitfalls and snares, weak knees, weary feet, and subtle enemies, no child of God would stand fast for an hour were it not for the faithful love which will not allow his foot to be moved.

"Amidst a thousand snares I stand upheld and guarded by Thy hand; that hand unseen shall hold me still, and lead me to Thy holy hill."

THE LORD'S FREE MEN

Sin shall not have dominion over you,
for you are not under law but under grace.

~ *Romans 6:14*

Sin will reign if it can: it cannot be satisfied with any place below the throne of the heart. But the Lord gives us this comforting assurance, "Sin shall not have dominion over you." It may assail you and even wound you, but it shall never establish sovereignty over you.

If we were under the law, our sin would gather strength and hold us under its power, but as we are under the covenant of grace, we are secured against departing from the living God by the sure declaration of the covenant. Grace is promised to us, by which we are restored from our wanderings, cleansed from our impurities, and set free from the chains of habit.

Since we are the Lord's people, we take courage to fight our corruptions and temptations, being assured that sin shall never bring us under its sway again. God Himself gives us the victory through Jesus Christ.

SANCTIFIED AND SATISFIED

"My people shall be satisfied with
My goodness, says the Lord."

~ *Jeremiah 31:14*

The kind of people who are satisfied with God are marked out as God's own. He is pleased with them, for they are pleased with Him. They call Him their God, and He calls them His people. There is a mutual communion of delight between God's Israel and Israel's God.

These people are satisfied. This is a grand thing. Very few of the sons of men are ever satisfied, let their lot be what it may. Only sanctified souls are satisfied souls. God Himself must both convert us and content us.

It is no wonder that the Lord's people should be satisfied with the goodness of their Lord. Here is goodness without mixture, mercy without chiding, love without change, favor without reserve.

If God's goodness does not satisfy us, what will? Surely there is a wrong desire within if it be one that God's goodness does not satisfy.

THE UNFAILING WATCH

Behold, He who keeps Israel shall
neither slumber nor sleep.

~ *Psalm 121:4*

Jehovah is "the Keeper of Israel." No form of unconsciousness ever steals over Him, neither the deeper slumber, nor the slighter sleep. He never fails to watch the house and the heart of His people. This is a sufficient reason for our resting in perfect peace. When we lie defenseless, Jehovah Himself will cover our head.

The Lord keeps His people as a rich man keeps his treasure, as a sentry keeps watch over his sovereign. None can harm those who are in such keeping. Let me put my soul into His dear hands. He never forgets us, never ceases actively to care for us, never finds Himself unable to preserve us.

O my Lord, keep me, lest I wander and fall and perish. Keep me, that I may keep Your commandments. By Your unslumbering care, prevent my sleeping like the sluggard and perishing like those who sleep the sleep of death.

THE NAME TO USE

*"If you ask anything in My name,
I will do it."*

~ *John 14:14*

Anything! Whether large or small, all my needs are covered by that word "anything."

What a wise promise! We are always to ask in the name of Jesus. While this encourages us, it also honors Him. The name of Jesus is as mighty at the throne as ever, and we may plead it with full assurance.

What an instructive prayer! I may not ask for anything to which I cannot put Christ's hand and seal. I dare not use my Lord's name to a selfish or willful petition. I may only use my Lord's name to prayers that He would Himself pray. It is a high privilege to be authorized to ask in the name of Jesus as if Jesus Himself asked.

Am I asking for that which Jesus approves? Dare I put His seal to my prayer? Then I have that which I seek of the Father.

LIMITLESS RICHES

*"My God shall supply all your need according
to His riches in glory by Christ Jesus."*

~ *Philippians 4:19*

Paul's God is our God, and He will supply all our need. God will do it, for He loves us, He delights to bless us, and it will glorify Him to do so. His pity, His power, His love, His faithfulness, all work together that we be not famished.

What a measure the Lord goes by, "According to His riches in glory by Christ Jesus." The riches of His grace are large, but what shall we say of the riches of His glory? Who shall form an estimate of this? According to this immeasurable measure will God fill up the immense abyss of our necessities. He makes the Lord Jesus the receptacle and the channel of His fullness, and then He imparts to us His wealth of love in its highest form. Hallelujah!

"My God shall supply all your need." God's supplies are surer than any bank.

WEAPONS DOOMED TO FAIL

*"No weapon formed against you shall prosper,
and every tongue which rises against you
in judgment you shall condemn."*

~ Isaiah 54:17

There is great clatter in the forges and smithies of the enemy. They are making weapons to smite the saints with. See how busily they labor! It matters nothing, for on the blade of every weapon you may read this inscription: *It shall not prosper.*

But now listen to another noise: it is the strife of tongues. Tongues are more terrible instruments than can be made with hammers and anvils, and the evil that they inflict cuts deeper and spreads wider. What will become of us now? Slander, falsehood, insinuation, ridicule – these are poisoned arrows; how can we meet them?

The Lord God promises us that, if we cannot silence them, we shall at least escape from being ruined by them. They condemn us for the moment, but we shall condemn them at last and forever. The mouth of falsehoods shall be turned to the honor of those good men who suffered by them.

GOD NEVER FORSAKES

*The LORD will not cast off His people,
nor will He forsake His inheritance.*

~ *Psalm 94:14*

Man has his cast-offs, but God has none; for His choice is unchangeable, and His love is everlasting. None can find a single person whom God has forsaken after having revealed Himself savingly to him.

The Lord chastens His own; but He never forsakes them. The ungodly are let alone till the pit is digged into which they will fall and be taken, but the godly are sent to school to be prepared for their glorious destiny hereafter. Judgment will return and finish its work upon the rebels, but it will equally return to vindicate the sincere and godly. Hence we may bear the rod of chastisement with calm submission; it means not anger, but love.

> God may chasten and correct,
> But He never can neglect;
> May in faithfulness reprove,
> But He ne'er can cease to love.

CLEARLY SUPERNATURAL

*In that day the Lord will defend the inhabitants
of Jerusalem; the one who is feeble among
them in that day shall be like David, and
the house of David shall be like God,
like the Angel of the Lord before them.*

~ *Zechariah 12:8*

One of the best methods of the Lord's defending His people is to make them strong in inward might.

The Lord can take the feeblest among us and make him like David, the champion of Israel. Lord, do this with me! Infuse Your power into me, and fill me with sacred courage that I may face the giant with sling and stone, confident in God.

The Lord can make His greatest champions far mightier than they are: Lord, show us what You are able to do – namely, to raise Your faithful servants to a height of grace and holiness which shall be clearly supernatural!

Lord, dwell in Your saints, put Your might into them, and they shall be as the living creatures who dwell in the presence of Jehovah. Fulfill this promise to Your entire church in this our day, for Jesus' sake. Amen.

FROM OBEDIENCE TO BLESSING

"From this day I will bless you."

~ *Haggai 2:19*

Future things are hidden from us. Yet here is a glass in which we may see the unborn years. The Lord says, "From this day I will bless you."

Note the day that is referred to in this promise. There had been failure of crops, blasting, and mildew – all because of the people's sin. Now, the Lord saw these chastened ones commencing to obey His word and build His temple, therefore He says, "From this day I will bless you."

If we have lived in any sin, and the Spirit leads us to purge ourselves of it, we may reckon upon the blessing of the Lord. His smile, His Spirit, His grace, His fuller revelation of His truth will all prove to us an enlarged blessing.

Lord, I am resolved to be more true to You and I pray, therefore, that You will increase the blessedness of my daily life henceforth and forever.

HUNGER SATISFIED

He satisfies the longing soul,
and fills the hungry soul with goodness.

~ *Psalm 107:9*

It is well to have longings, and the more intense they are the better. The Lord will satisfy soul longings, however great and all-absorbing they may be. Let us greatly long, for God will greatly give. Blessed Spirit, make us sigh and cry after better things, and for more of the best things!

Hunger is by no means a pleasant sensation. Yet blessed are they that hunger and thirst after righteousness. Such persons shall not only have their hunger relieved with a little food, but they shall be filled with goodness by Jehovah Himself.

Come, let us not fret because we long and hunger, but let us hear the voice of the psalmist as he also longs and hungers to see God magnified. "Oh, that men would give thanks to the LORD for His goodness, and for His wonderful works to the children of men!" (Ps. 107:8).

THE OUTWARD, UPWARD LOOK

"Look to Me, and be saved, all you ends of the earth!
For I am God, and there is no other."

~ Isaiah 45:22

This is a promise of promises. It lies at the foundation of our spiritual life. How simple is the direction! "Look to Me." We have looked elsewhere long enough; it is time to look to Him who invites our expectation and promises to give us His salvation.

Only a look! Will we not look at once? We are to bring nothing in ourselves but to look upward to God. A look requires no preparation, no violent effort. It needs neither wit nor wisdom, wealth nor strength. All that we need is in the Lord, and if we look to Him for everything, that everything shall be ours, and we shall be saved.

Come, look hither! As from the furthest regions men may see the sun and enjoy his light, so you who lie in death's borders at the very gates of hell may by a look receive the salvation of the Lord Jesus Christ.

NO CONDEMNATION

"In those days and in that time," says the LORD,
*"The iniquity of Israel shall be sought,
but there shall be none; and the sins of Judah,
but they shall not be found;
for I will pardon those whom I preserve."*

~ *Jeremiah 50:20*

A glorious word indeed! What a perfect pardon is here promised! Sin is to be so removed that it shall not be found, so blotted out that there shall be none. Glory be to the God of pardons!

Satan seeks out sins to accuse us with, our enemies seek them that they may lay them to our charge, and even our own conscience seeks them. But when the Lord applies the precious blood of Jesus, we fear no form of search, for "there shall be none," "They shall not be found." The sacrifice of Jesus has cast our sins into the depths of the sea. This makes us dance for joy.

The reason for the obliteration of sin lies in the fact that Jehovah Himself pardons His chosen ones. He speaks absolution, and we are absolved. Blessed be the name of the sin-annihilating God!

ACQUIRING PERSEVERANCE

*The LORD your God will drive out those nations
before you little by little.*

~ Deuteronomy 7:22

Do not expect to win victories for the Lord by a single blow. Evil principles and practices die hard. In some places it takes years of labor to drive out even one vice. Yet we must carry on the war with all our might, even when favored with little manifest success.

Our business in this world is to conquer it for Jesus. We are not to seek popularity, but to wage unceasing war with iniquity.

The Lord our God can alone accomplish this, and He promises that He will so work. This He will do by degrees, that we may learn perseverance, may increase in faith, may earnestly watch, and may avoid carnal security. Let us thank God for a little success and pray for more. Let us never sheathe the sword till the whole land is won for Jesus.

Go on little by little, for many "littles" will make a great whole.

PARDON AND FORGIVENESS

*"He will not always chide: neither
will He keep His anger for ever."*

~ *Psalm 103:9 KJV*

He will chide sometimes, or He would not be a wise Father for such poor erring children as we are. We know what this chiding means, and we bow before the Lord, mourning that we should cause Him to be angry with us.

But what a comfort we find in these lines! "Not always" will He chide. If we repent and turn to Him with hearts broken *for* sin and broken *from* sin, He will smile upon us at once. It is no pleasure to Him to turn a frowning face toward those whom He loves with all His heart: it is His joy that our joy should be full.

Come, let us seek His face. There is no reason for despair, or even for despondency. He who pardoned us long ago as a judge will again forgive us as a father, and we shall rejoice in His sweet, unchanging love.

MOUNTAINS TURNED TO PLAINS

Who are you, O great mountain?
Before Zerubbabel you shall become a plain!
And he shall bring forth the capstone with shouts of
"Grace, grace to it!"

~ Zechariah 4:7

At this hour a mountain of difficulty or distress may be in our way, and natural reason sees no path over it, through it, or around it. Let faith come in, and straightaway the mountain becomes a plain. But faith must first hear the word of the Lord, "Not by might nor by power, but by My Spirit" (Zech. 4:6).

This grand truth is necessary for meeting the insurmountable trials of life. I see that I can do nothing, and that all reliance on man is vanity. "Not by might." God alone must work.

If the Almighty God takes up the concerns of His people, then great mountains are nothing. He can remove worlds as boys toss balls about. This power He can lend to me. If the Lord bids me move an Alp, I can do it through His name. What can I be afraid of with God on my side?

HEAVENLY ALCHEMY

"Your sorrow will be turned into joy."

~ *John 16:20*

The more sorrow, the more joy. If we have loads of sorrow, then the Lord's power will turn them into tons of joy. The bitterer the trouble, the sweeter the pleasure. The swinging of the pendulum far to the left will cause it to go farther to the right. The remembrance of the grief shall heighten the flavor of the delight.

Come, my heart, cheer up! In a little while I shall be as glad as I am now gloomy. Jesus tells me that by a heavenly alchemy, my sorrow shall be turned into joy. I do not see how it is to be, but I believe it, and I begin to sing by way of anticipation.

This depression of spirit is not for long; I shall soon be up among the happy ones who praise the Lord day and night, and there I shall sing of the mercy that delivered me out of great afflictions.

REST IN ALL YOUR GOINGS

And He said, "My Presence will go with you,
and I will give you rest."

~ Exodus 33:14

Precious promise! Lord, enable me to appropriate it as all my own.

It often happens that when we feel most at home in a place, we are suddenly called away from it. Here is the antidote for this ill. The Lord Himself will keep us company. His presence, which includes His favor, His fellowship, His care, and His power, shall be ever with us in every one of our marchings. If we have God present with us, we have possession of heaven and earth.

Go with me, Lord, and command me where You wish! But we hope to find a place of rest. The text promises it.

God's presence will cause us to rest even when we are on the march, even in the midst of battle. To be with God is to rest in the most emphatic sense.

DOING WHAT GOD CAN BLESS

*The LORD will command the blessing on you
in your storehouses and in all to which you set your hand.*

~ Deuteronomy 28:8

If we obey the Lord our God, He will bless that which He gives us. Riches are no curse when blessed of the Lord. When men have more than they require for their immediate need and begin to lay up in storehouses, the dry rot of covetousness or the blight of hard-heartedness is apt to follow the accumulation; but with God's blessing, it is not so. Prudence arranges the saving, liberality directs the spending, gratitude maintains consecration, and praise sweetens enjoyment.

The Lord will bless all that you "set your hand" to. We would not put our hand to anything upon which we dare not ask God's blessing, neither would we go about it without prayer and faith. But what a privilege to be able to look for the Lord's help in every enterprise!

The Lord's blessing is infinitely more than all the fruit of talent, genius, or tact.

KNOW HOW TO WAIT

"Whoever believes will not act hastily."

~ Isaiah 28:16

Make haste to keep the Lord's commandments; but do not make haste in any impatient or improper sense.

When others are flying hither and thither as if their wits had failed them, the believer shall be quiet, calm, and deliberate, and so shall be able to act wisely in the hour of trial. He shall not haste in his expectations, craving his good things at once and on the spot; but he will wait God's time. He shall not haste by plunging into wrong or questionable action.

Faith makes no more haste than good speed, and thus it is not forced to go back sorrowfully by the way which it followed heedlessly.

How is it with me? Am I believing, and therefore, keeping to the believer's pace, which is walking with God? Peace, fluttering spirit! Rest in the Lord, and wait patiently for Him!

GOD IS IN THE FRONT LINE

He is the One who goes before you.
He will be with you, He will not leave you
nor forsake you; do not fear nor be dismayed.

~ Deuteronomy 31:8

This text should help us to buckle on our harness in warfare. If Jehovah Himself goes before us, it must be safe to follow. Come, let us make a prompt advance! Why do we hesitate to pass on to victory?

Nor is the Lord before us only; He is with us – above, beneath, around, within.

Being before us and with us, He will never withdraw His help. He cannot fail in Himself, and He will not fail toward us. He will continue to help us according to our need, even to the end.

As He cannot fail us, so He will not forsake us. He will always be both able and willing to grant us strength.

Let us not fear nor be dismayed; for the Lord of hosts will go down to the battle with us, will bear the brunt of the fight, and give us the victory.

December

TRUE WALKING POSTURE

He who walks with integrity walks securely.

~ Proverbs 10:9

His walk may be slow, but it is sure. He that hastens to be rich shall not be innocent or sure; but steady perseverance in integrity, if it does not bring riches, will certainly bring peace.

In doing that which is just and right, we are like one walking upon a rock, for we have confidence that every step we take is upon solid and safe ground. The man who has gained success through questionable transactions must always be afraid that a day of reckoning will come.

Let us stick to truth and righteousness. Never, on any account whatsoever, let us do that which our conscience cannot justify. If we keep in the Lord's own way, and never sin against our conscience, our way is sure against all.

We may be thought fools for being firm in our integrity; but in the place where judgment is infallible, we shall be approved.

OUR HOLIEST EXAMPLE

I have set the LORD always before me; because
He is at my right hand I shall not be moved.

~ *Psalm 16:8*

This is the way to live. With God always before us, we shall have the noblest companionship, the holiest example, the sweetest consolation, and the mightiest influence.

Always to have an eye to the Lord's eye, and an ear for the Lord's voice – this is the right state for the godly man. His God is near him, filling the horizon of his vision, leading the way of his life, and furnishing the theme of his meditation.

What vanities we should avoid, what sins we should overcome, what virtues we should exhibit, what joys we should experience if we did indeed set the Lord always before us!

The Lord, being ever in our minds, guides and aids us, and hence we are not moved by fear, or force, or fraud, or fickleness. When God stands at a man's right hand, that man is himself sure to stand.

PEACE WHATEVER EXPOSURE

> *"I will make a covenant of peace with them,*
> *and cause wild beasts to cease from the land;*
> *and they will dwell safely in the wilderness*
> *and sleep in the woods."*

> ~ Ezekiel 34:25

It is the height of grace that Jehovah should be in covenant with man, a feeble, sinful creature. Yet the Lord has solemnly entered into a faithful covenant with us, and from that covenant He will never turn aside. In virtue of this covenant we are safe. As lions and wolves are driven off by shepherds, so shall all noxious influences be chased away. The Lord will give us rest from disturbers and destroyers.

The Lord's people are to enjoy security in places of the greatest exposure: wilderness and woods are to be as pastures and folds to the flock of Christ. If the Lord does not change the place for the better, He will make us the better in the place.

Nothing without or within should cause any fear to the child of God. By faith the wilderness can become the suburbs of heaven, and the woods the vestibule of glory.

COVERED AND PROTECTED

He shall cover you with His feathers,
and under His wings you shall take refuge;
His truth shall be your shield and buckler.

~ *Psalm 91:4*

Just as a hen protects her brood and allows them to nestle under her wings, so will the Lord defend His people and permit them to hide away in Him. Have we not seen the little chicks peeping out from under the mother's feathers and heard their little cries of contented joy? In this way let us shelter ourselves in our God, and feel overflowing peace in knowing that He is guarding us. While the Lord covers us, we trust.

When we go out to war in His name we enjoy the same guardian care. When we implicitly trust God, even as the chick trusts the hen, we find His truth arming us from head to foot. The Lord cannot lie; He must be faithful to His people; His promise must stand. This sure truth is all the shield we need.

Come, my soul, hide under those great wings, lose yourself among those soft feathers!

HIGH PLACES OF DEFENSE

He will dwell on high; his place of defense
will be the fortress of rocks; bread will
be given him, his water will be sure.

~ Isaiah 33:16

The man to whom God has given grace to be of blameless life dwells in perfect security. He dwells on high, above the world, out of reach of the enemy, and near to heaven.

He is defended by munitions of stupendous rock. The firmest things in the universe are the promise and purposes of the unchanging God, and these the safeguard of the obedient believer.

He is provided for by this great promise, "Bread shall be given him." The Lord, who rained manna in the wilderness, will keep His people in good store even when they are surrounded by those who would starve them.

But what if water should fail? That cannot be "his waters shall be sure." The Lord sees that nothing is wanting. None can touch the citizen of the true Zion. However fierce the enemy, the Lord will preserve His chosen.

THROUGH, NOT ENGULFED

*"When you pass through the waters, I will be with you;
and through the rivers, they shall not overflow you.
When you walk through the fire, you shall not
be burned, nor shall the flame scorch you."*

~ *Isaiah 43:2*

Bridge there is none: we must go through the waters, and feel the rush of the rivers. Tried we must be, but triumphant we shall be; for Jehovah Himself, who is mightier than many waters, shall be with us. The Lord will surely be with us in difficulties and dangers. The sorrows of life may rise to an extraordinary height, but the Lord is equal to every occasion.

The enemies of God can put dangers in our way but we shall walk through the fires. God being with us, we shall not be burned or smell of smoke.

Oh, the wonderful security of the heaven-born and heaven-bound pilgrim! Floods cannot drown him, nor fires burn him. Your presence, Lord, is the protection of Your saints from the varied perils of the road. In faith I commit myself unto You, and my spirit enters into rest.

GIFT OF STRENGTH, PEACE TO BLESS

The LORD will give strength to His people;
the LORD will bless His people with peace.

~ Psalm 29:11

David had just heard the voice of the Lord in a thunderstorm, and had seen His power in the hurricane; and now, in the cool calm after the storm, that overwhelming power by which heaven and earth are shaken is promised to be the strength of the chosen.

Why are we weak when we have divine strength to flee to? Why are we troubled when the Lord's own peace is ours? Jesus, the mighty God, is our strength; let us put Him on and go forth to our services. Jesus, our blessed Lord, is also our peace; let us repose in Him this day and end our fears.

That same God who rides upon the storm in days of tempest will also rule the hurricane of our tribulation and send us, before long, days of peace. We shall have strength for storms and songs for fair weather. Away, dark thoughts! Up, faith and hope!

FOLLOWING LEADS TO HONOR

"If anyone serves Me, let him follow Me;
and where I am, there My servant will be also.
If anyone serves Me, him My Father will honor."

~ John 12:26

To do as Jesus did is the surest way of bringing honor to His name. Let me mind this every day.

If I imitate Jesus, I shall have His company; if I am like Him, I shall be with Him. In due time He will take me up to dwell with Him above, if I have striven to follow Him here below. After His suffering our Lord came to His throne, and, after we have suffered a while with Him here below, we also shall arrive in glory. Come, my soul, pluck up courage.

Let me not fail to note that the Father will honor those who follow His Son. If He sees me true to Jesus, He will put marks of favor and honor upon me for His Son's sake.

No honor can be like this; the substance of glory comes from the Father. Therefore, cling to the Lord more closely than ever.

THE "ALL" OF BELIEF

Jesus said to him, "If you can believe,
all things are possible to him who believes."

~ Mark 9:23

Our unbelief is the greatest hindrance in our way.
The Lord can do everything, but when He makes a
rule that according to our faith so shall it be unto us,
our unbelief ties the hands of His omnipotence.

God is always true; why do we not believe Him?
He is always faithful to His Word; why can we not
trust Him? When we are in a right state of heart,
faith costs no effort: it is then as natural for us to rely
upon God as for a child to trust its father.

The worst of it is that we can believe God about
everything except the present pressing trial. This is
folly. Shake off such sinfulness, and trust God with
the load, the labor, the longing of this present. This
done, all is done.

GOD IS OUR ALLY

*"If you indeed obey His voice and do all that I speak,
then I will be an enemy to your enemies
and an adversary to your adversaries."*

~ *Exodus 23:22*

Jesus Christ is to be acknowledged and obeyed. He is the vicegerent of God and speaks in the Father's name, and it is our responsibility to do as He commands. We shall lose the promise if we disregard the precept.

The Lord enters into a league with His people. He will bless those who bless us, and curse those who curse us. God will go heart and soul with His people. We need not concern ourselves about our adversaries when we are assured that they have become the adversaries of God.

So far as our own interest is concerned, we have no enemies; but for the cause of truth and righteousness, we take up arms and go forth to conflict.

We are allied with the eternal God; and if we carefully obey the law of our Lord Jesus, He is engaged to put forth all His power on our behalf.

TRUST AND DO; DO AND TRUST

*Trust in the LORD, and do good; dwell
in the land, and feed on His faithfulness.*

~ Psalm 37:3

Trust and *do* are words that go well together. We should have faith, and that faith should work. We do not sit still because we trust, but we arouse ourselves and expect the Lord to work through us and by us. It is ours to trust and do good. We neither trust without doing, nor do without trusting.

Adversaries would root us out if they could; but by trusting and doing, we dwell in the land. We are not so easily to be got rid of as the Lord's enemies suppose. Where God has given us a name and a place, there we abide.

But what about the supply of our necessities? As sure as God is true, His people shall be fed. It is theirs to trust and to do, and it is the Lord's to do according to their trust. They shall be fed somehow. Away, fears!

A QUIET HEART

*"In quietness and confidence
shall be your strength."*

~ Isaiah 30:15

It is weakness to be fretting and worrying, questioning and mistrusting. Do we not unfit ourselves for action, and unhinge our minds for wise decision? We are sinking by our struggles when we might float by faith.

Oh, for grace to be quiet! Why run from house to house repeating the weary story that makes us more and more heartsick as we tell it? Why stay at home to cry out in agony because of wretched forebodings that may never by fulfilled? Be still and know that Jehovah is God!

Oh, for grace to be confident in God! Every word of His will stand though the mountains should depart. He deserves to be confided in; and if we would display confidence and consequent quietness, we might be as happy as the spirits before the throne. Return unto your rest, and lean your head upon the Lord Jesus.

EVENING BRIGHTENS INTO DAY

*At evening time it shall happen
that it will be light.*

~ *Zechariah 14:7*

It is a surprise that it should be so; but God is wont to work in a way so that the dark will not deepen into midnight, but will suddenly brighten into day. Never let us despair. In the worst times let us trust in the Lord who turns the darkness of the shadow of death into the morning.

This promise should assist our patience. The light may not fully come till our hopes are quite quite spent by waiting all day to no purpose. But to the righteous, the sun rises when it is almost night. May we not with patience wait for that heavenly light, which may be long in coming, but is sure to prove itself well worth waiting for?

Come, my soul, sing unto Him who will bless you in life and in death, in a manner surpassing all that nature has ever seen when at its best.

NOTHING OLD

He who sat on the throne said,
"Behold, I make all things new."

~ Revelation 21:5

All things need making new, for they are sadly battered and worn by sin. But no one can make all things new except God, who made them at the first. Our Lord Jesus has undertaken the task, and He is fully competent for the performance of it.

Already He has commenced His labor, and for centuries He has persevered in making new the hearts of men. And there shall come a day when the body shall be made new and raised like unto His glorious body.

What a joy to belong to a kingdom where everything is being made new! We are not dying out: we are hastening on to a more glorious life. Despite the opposition of the powers of evil, our glorious Lord Jesus is accomplishing His purpose and making us, and all about us, "new," and as full of beauty as when they first came from the hand of the Lord.

WORLD CONCORD

They shall beat their swords into plowshares,
and their spears into pruning hooks;
nation shall not lift up sword against nation,
neither shall they learn war anymore.

~ Isaiah 2:4

Oh, that these happy times were come! At present the nations are heavily armed and are inventing weapons more and more terrible. Yet peace will prevail one day; yes, and so prevail that the instruments of destruction shall be beaten into other shapes and used for better purposes.

How will this come about? Lasting peace will be established only by the reign of the Prince of Peace. He must teach the people by His Spirit, renew their hearts by His grace, and reign over them by His supreme power; and then will they cease to wound and kill.

Let every reader of this book of promises offer special prayer today to the Lord and Giver of Peace, that He would speedily put an end to war and establish concord over the whole world.

DIVINE EXPULSION

*You shall drive out the Canaanites, though
they have iron chariots and are strong.*

~ Joshua 17:18

It is a great encouragement to be assured of victory, for then a man goes to war in confidence. Our warfare is with evil within us and around us, and we ought to be persuaded that we are able to get the victory in the name of the Lord Jesus. We are not riding for a fall, but to win; and win we shall.

Certain of our sins find chariots of iron in our constitution – our former habits, associations, and occupations. They are very strong, yet in the name of God we must master them, and we will.

If one sin has dominion of us, we are not the Lord's free men. A man who is held by only one chain is still a captive. Up, then, and break to shivers every chariot of iron! The Lord of Hosts is with us, and who shall resist His sin-destroying power?

NEAREST AND DEAREST FELLOWSHIP

We shall always be with the Lord.

~ 1 Thessalonians 4:17

While we are here the Lord is with us, and when we are called away we are with Him. There is no dividing the saints from the Savior. They are one, and they always must be one: Jesus cannot be without His own people.

What a joy is this! Our supreme honor, rest, comfort, delight, is to be with the Lord. We cannot conceive of anything that can surpass or even equal this divine society. Before long we shall be with Him in His rest and in His royalty, in His expectation and in His manifestation.

Lord, if I am to be forever with You, I have a destiny incomparable. To be forever with the Lord is my idea of heaven at its best. Not the harps of gold, not the crowns unfading, nor the light unclouded, is glory to me; but Jesus, and myself forever with Him in nearest and dearest fellowship.

DEFENDED AND COVERED

*Like birds flying about, so will
the LORD of hosts defend Jerusalem.*

~ Isaiah 31:5

With hurrying wing the mother bird hastens to the protection of her young. She wastes no time when coming to supply them with food or guard them from danger. Thus as on eagles' wings will the Lord come to the defense of His chosen.

With outspread wing, the mother covers her little ones in the nest and makes her wings a house for them to dwell. Thus God Himself becomes the protection of His elect. He Himself is their refuge, their abode, their all.

As birds flying, and birds covering (for the word means both), so will the Lord be unto us. We shall be defended and preserved from all evil: the Lord who likens Himself to birds will not be like them in their feebleness, for He is Jehovah.

The wing of God is quicker and tenderer than the wing of a bird, and we will put our trust under its shadow.

AFFLICTIONS, BUT
NO BROKEN BONES

He guards all his bones;
not one of them is broken.

~ *Psalm 34:20*

This is great comfort to a tried child of God, and comfort which I dare accept, for up to this hour have offered no real damage from my many afflictions. I have neither lost faith, nor hope, nor love. Nay, so far from losing these bones of character, they have gained in strength and energy.

I have more knowledge, more experience, more patience, more stability than I had before the trials came. Not even my joy has been destroyed. Many a bruise have I had by sickness, bereavement, depression, slander, and opposition, but the bruise has healed. The reason is not far to seek. If we trust in the Lord, He keeps all our bones; and if He keeps them, we may be sure that not one of them is broken.

Come, my heart, do not sorrow. There are no bones broken. Endure hardness, and bid defiance to fear.

MEN AS MEN, GOD AS GOD

*"I, even I, am He who comforts you. Who are you
that you should be afraid of a man who will die,
and of the son of a man who will be made like grass?
And you forget the LORD your Maker, who stretched
out the heavens and laid the foundations of the earth;
you have feared continually every day because of
the fury of the oppressor, when he has prepared to
destroy. And where is the fury of the oppressor?"*

~ Isaiah 51:12-13

Let the text itself be taken as the portion for today.
Read it, believe it, feed on it, and plead it before the
Lord. He whom you fear is only a man; while He
who promises to comfort you is God, your Maker,
and the Creator of heaven and earth.

"Where is the fury of the oppressor?" It is in the
Lord's hand. It is only the fury of a dying creature,
fury that will end as soon as the breath is gone from
the nostril. Why, then, should we stand in awe of
one who is as frail as ourselves? Let us not dishonor
our God by making a god of puny man. Let us treat
men as men, and God as God; and then we shall go
calmly on in the path of duty, fearing the Lord, and
fearing nobody else.

FROM ANGER TO LOVE

*He will again have compassion on us, and
will subdue our iniquities. You will cast all
our sins into the depths of the sea.*

~ Micah 7:19

God never turns from His love, but He soon turns from His wrath. His love to His chosen is according to His nature; His anger is only according to His office: He loves because He is love; He frowns because it is necessary for our good. He will come back to the place where His heart rests; namely, His love for His own, and then He will take pity upon our griefs and end them.

What a promise is this, "He will subdue our iniquities!" He will conquer them. They cry to enslave us, but the Lord will give us victory over them.

As for the guilt for our sins, how gloriously is that removed! "All our sins" – yes, all of them; "You will cast" – only an almighty arm could perform such a wonder; "into the depths of the sea." They are all gone. They sank into the bottom like a stone. Hallelujah!

IMMEDIATELY PRESENT

God is our refuge and strength,
a very present help in trouble.

~ *Psalm 46:1*

Help that is not present when we need it is of small value. The anchor that is left at home is of no use to the seaman in the hour of storm. Very few earthly helps could be called "very present."

They are usually far in the seeking and far in the using. But the Lord is present when we seek Him, present when we need Him, and present when we have already enjoyed His aid.

He is more than "present." He is very present: more present than the nearest friend can be, for He is in us in our trouble.

He is our refuge; let us hide in Him. He is our strength; let us array ourselves with Him. He is our help; let us lean upon Him. He is our very present help; let us repose in Him now. We need not have a moment's care or an instant's fear.

PRECIOUS THINGS

*Of Joseph he said: "Blessed of the LORD is his land,
with the precious things of heaven,
with the dew, and the deep lying beneath."*

~ *Deuteronomy 33:13*

Oh, for "the precious things of heaven"! Power with God, and the manifestation of power from God, is most precious. We would enjoy the peace of God, the joy of the Lord, the glory of our God. The benediction of the three divine Persons in love and grace and fellowship, we prize beyond the finest gold. The things of earth are as nothing in preciousness compared with the things of heaven.

"The dew." What refreshing, what growth, what perfume, what life there is in us when the dew is about! Above all things, as plants of the Lord's, we need the dew of His Holy Spirit.

"The deep lying beneath." Surely this refers to that unseen ocean underground which supplies all the fresh springs which make glad the earth. Oh to tap the eternal fountains! This is an unspeakable blessing; let no believer rest till he possesses it.

OVER JORDAN WITH SINGING

Your enemies shall submit to you.

~ Deuteronomy 33:29

That archenemy, the devil, is a liar from the beginning; but he is so very plausible that, like Eve, we are led to believe him. Yet in our experience we shall prove him a liar.

He says that we shall fall from grace, dishonor our profession, and perish with the doom of apostates; but, trusting in the Lord, we shall hold onto our way and prove that Jesus loses none whom His Father gave Him. He tells us that our bread will fail, and we shall starve; yet the Feeder of the ravens has not forgotten us yet, and He will prepare us a table in the presence of our enemies. He whispers that the Lord will not deliver us out of our trial. What a liar he is! The Lord will never leave us, nor forsake us.

The devil takes great delight in telling us that death will prove too much for us. "How will you do in the floodplain of the Jordan?" But there also he shall prove a liar unto us, and we shall pass through the river singing psalms of glory.

HE CAME; HE IS COMING

*This same Jesus, who was taken up from you into heaven,
will so come in like manner as you
saw Him go into heaven.*

~ Acts 1:11

Many are celebrating our Lord's first coming this day; let us turn our thoughts to the promise of His Second Coming. He who came to suffer will not be slow in coming to reign.

This is our glorious hope, for we shall share His joy. Today we are in our concealment and humiliation, even as He was while here below; but when He comes it will be our manifestation, even as it will be His revelation.

The slandered and despised shall shine forth as the sun in the kingdom of their Father. The long rest and inconceivable splendor of the millennial reign will be an abundant recompense for the ages of witnessing and warring.

He is coming! He is on the road and traveling quickly. The sound of His approach should be as music to our hearts! Ring out, you bells of hope!

TRUST ONLY IN GOD

*Peter answered and said to Him, "Even if all
are made to stumble because of You,
I will never be made to stumble."*

~ Matthew 26:33

Peter thought that he was saying what he should assuredly carry out, but a promise that has no better foundation than a human resolve will fall to the ground. No sooner did temptations arise than Peter denied his Master and used oaths to confirm his denial.

What is man's word? An earthen pot broken with a stroke. What is your own resolve? A blossom, which, with God's care, may come to fruit, but which, left to itself, will fall to the ground with the first wind that moves the bough.

On man's word hang only what it will bear.

On your own resolve depend not at all.

On the promise of God hang time and eternity, this world and the next, your all and the all of your beloved ones.

Rely upon Jesus without limit. Trust not yourself or any man beyond due bounds, but trust only and wholly in the Lord.

HIS KINDNESS AND COVENANT

"The mountains shall depart and the hills be removed,
but My kindness shall not depart from you,
nor shall My covenant of peace be removed,"
says the LORD, *who has mercy on you.*

~ *Isaiah 54:10*

One of the most delightful qualities of divine love is its abiding character. The pillars of the earth may be moved out of their places, but the kindness and the covenant of our merciful Jehovah never depart from His people. The year is almost over, and the years of life are growing few, but time does not change my Lord; our Lord is the same. Force overturns the hills, but no conceivable power can affect the eternal God. Nothing in the past, the present, or the future can cause Jehovah to be unkind to me.

My soul, rest in the *eternal kindness* of the Lord. Remember also the *everlasting covenant*. God is ever mindful of it; see that you are mindful of it too. Kindness and covenant – dwell on these words, assure and lasting things which eternity itself shall not take from you.

ABSOLUTE ASSURANCE

He Himself has said,
"I will never leave you nor forsake you."

~ Hebrews 13:5

Several times in the Scriptures the Lord has said this. Let us never harbor a doubt of it. In itself the promise is especially emphatic. In the Greek it has five negatives, each one definitely shutting out the possibility of the Lord's ever leaving one of His people.

This priceless Scripture does not promise us exemption from trouble, but it does secure us against desertion. We may be called to traverse strange ways, but we shall always have our Lord's company, assistance, and provision. His favor is better than fortune.

We ought surely to be content with such things as we have, for he who has God has more than all the world besides. What can we have beyond the Infinite?

If God says He will never leave you nor forsake you, be much in prayer for grace, that you may never leave Him, nor even for a moment forsake His ways.

HE WILL CARRY US HOME

*"Even to your old age, I am He, and even to gray hairs
I will carry you! I have made, and I will bear;
even I will carry, and will deliver you."*

~ *Isaiah 46:4*

The year is very old, and here is a promise for us all, as age creeps over us. Let us live long enough, and we shall all have gray hairs; therefore we may as well enjoy this promise by the foresight of faith.

When we grow old, our God will still be the I AM, abiding evermore the same. Hoar hairs tell of our decay, but He decays not. When we cannot carry a burden and can hardly carry ourselves, the Lord will carry us.

He made us, and He will care for us. When we become a burden to our friends and a burden to ourselves, the Lord will not shake us off, rather He will take us up and carry and deliver us more fully than ever. Let us not dread old age. Let us grow old graciously, since the Lord Himself is with us in fullness of grace.

LOVED TO PERFECTION

> *"Having loved His own who were in the world,*
> *He loved them to the end."*
>
> *~ John 13:1*

"Having loved …" That He should ever have loved men at all is the marvel. What was there in His poor disciples that He should love them? What is there in me?

It is His nature to love. Love made the saints "His own"! He purchased them with blood and they became His treasure. Being His own, He will not lose them. Being His beloved, He will not cease to love them. He will not cease to love you!

"To the end," even till His death the ruling passion of love to His own reigned in His sacred bosom. It means also to the uttermost. He could not love them more: He gave Himself for them. Some read it, "to perfection." Truly He lavished upon them a perfect love, which had no flaw nor failure, no unwisdom, no unfaithfulness, and no reserve.

Such is the love of Jesus to each one of His people.

No Stranger in Heaven

You will guide me with Your counsel,
and afterward receive me to glory.

~ Psalm 73:24

From day to day and from year to year, my faith believes in the wisdom and love of God, and I know that I shall not believe in vain. No good word of His has ever failed, and I am sure that none shall ever fall to the ground.

I put myself into His hand for guidance. I know not the way that I should choose: the Lord shall choose mine inheritance for me. I need counsel and advice, for my duties are intricate and my condition is involved. The counsel of the infallible God I seek, in preference to my own judgment or the advice of friends.

Soon the end will come: a few more years, and I must depart out of this world unto the Father. My Lord will be near my bed. He will meet me at heaven's gate: He will welcome me to the Glory Land. I shall not be a stranger in heaven: my own God and Father will receive me to its endless bliss.

Glory be to Him
who will guide me here,
and receive me hereafter.
                    Amen.